Echoes of
TEXAS
FOOTBALL

Echoes of
TEXAS
FOOTBALL

The Greatest Stories Ever Told

Edited by Ken Samelson

TRIUMPH
B O O K S
CHICAGO

Library of Congress Cataloging-in-Publication Data

Echoes of Texas football : the greatest stories ever told / edited by Ken Samelson.
    p. cm.
Includes bibliographical references.
ISBN-13: 978-1-57243-763-0 (alk. paper)
ISBN-10: 1-57243-763-4 (alk. paper)
    1. Texas Longhorns (Football team)—History. 2. University of Texas at Austin—Football—History. I. Samelson, Ken.

GV958.T45E34 2006
796.332'630976431—dc22

2006014328

This book is available in quantity at special discounts for your group or organization. For further information, contact:

Triumph Books
542 South Dearborn Street
Suite 750
Chicago, Illinois 60605
(312) 939-3330
Fax (312) 663-3557

Printed in U.S.A.
ISBN-13: 978-1-57243-763-0
ISBN-10: 1-57243-763-4
Design by Patricia Frey
Photos courtesy of AP/Wide World Photos

CONTENTS

FOREWORD

I was watching the national champion Longhorns baseball team play last season when it occurred to me what a special fraternity the Texas Longhorns football program is. Coach Darrell Royal was at the baseball game, and everyone in the stands was interested in talking to him, even though he retired in 1976. There's a lot of pride in saying that I played for such a great coach and for a school like Texas, and it's a pride that all Longhorns fans share. That pride has only deepened in watching the exploits of the 2005 Longhorns.

All the athletes who were associated with Coach Royal at the time were living a dream, and it was a great opportunity. It's important that today's players understand how important it is to be a Longhorn and to make the most of it. Vince Young and Co. have done just that.

One of the greatest moves Coach Mack Brown made was to reunite the members of the football family who have played for the University of Texas. He brought back the tradition, which has always been there, but had receded a little bit. That has helped build on the foundation and has made the family stronger.

Being a Longhorn is a feeling of pride unlike any other.

Some of my greatest memories as a Longhorn include the opportunity to play in the Texas-Arkansas games and against Notre Dame in the 1970 Cotton Bowl. Notre Dame was coming out of retirement, so to speak, to play in the bowl game (the Irish hadn't played in a bowl since 1925), and their name was synonymous with college football back then. They were the only team you could watch on Sundays; the Fighting Irish's games were replayed on that day. So it was especially meaningful to win that game 21–17 in a thrilling comeback to complete an unbeaten national championship season.

Today, I'm delighted that the 2005 Longhorns will have similar memories to cherish.

I have great memories of my time at Texas, but what's especially amazing to me is how many people remember the things I did while I was a Longhorn. It was just a neat experience. As I have gotten older, I've realized just how lucky I was and how everything fell into place for me. I got to meet President Nixon after the Arkansas game in 1969 and President Johnson after the Notre Dame game that year. Later on, I went to Las Vegas and had the good fortune to meet Elvis backstage and Bill Medley of the Righteous Brothers. (Elvis said Texas deserved to beat Arkansas, while Bill Medley said he wanted Arkansas to win. I always was an Elvis fan!)

There is a lot of pride when you become a Longhorn. When you come to UT, you have access to a network of people for the rest of your life, whether you were a starter or not. When you go out to the business world, being a Longhorn means a lot. People always want to talk about my playing days and what's going on these days. My time at Texas opened several doors for me, and it continues to do so 30 years later.

I look back, and it all seems like it was a fairy tale or someone else's life. I'm thankful for the memories and everything UT has done for me.

And today, I'm so proud of the 2005 Longhorns for adding a special chapter to the history of Texas football.

—James Street

Echoes of
TEXAS
FOOTBALL

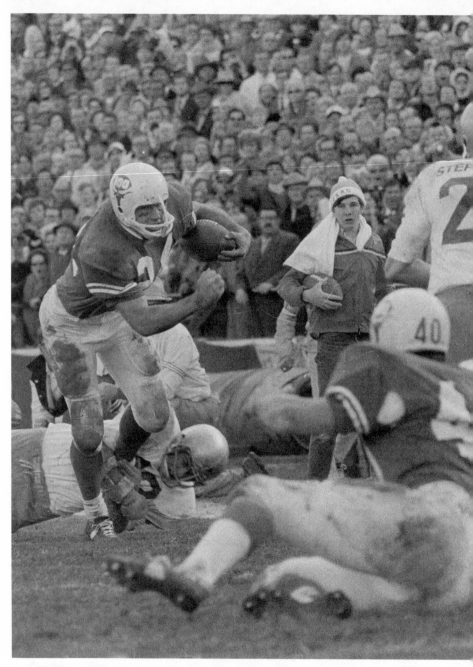

Ted Koy, University of Texas's star halfback, skirts through a bunch of fallen players to score from the 3-yard line in the Longhorns' Cotton Bowl victory over Notre Dame on January 1, 1970.

Section I
THE GAMES

Bill Little, *Texas Media Relations*

THE PLAY THAT CHANGED THE FACE OF TEXAS FOOTBALL

There might have been bigger Texas-Arkansas games through the years, but a good case can be made that the Longhorns' victory in 1939, led by Cowboy Jack Crain's heroics, might have been one of the most significant of them all. Previewing the 2003 Texas–Arkansas game, Bill Little took a look back at that historical game.

As a kid in the 1960s, Mack Brown grew up watching college football on TV with his dad and granddad.

So it was in that spirit and tradition that he urged the scheduling of this current two-game series between Texas and Arkansas. In the 1960s, there were no two greater figures in college football than Darrell Royal of Texas and Frank Broyles of Arkansas.

The two were the dominant figures in coaching in this part of the country, and despite their battles on the field, they were, and remain, close friends. So Saturday morning, for the first time since they both retired here in Austin in 1976, the two will appear on the field in the stadium which now shares Royal's name.

As they walk to midfield with their respective game captains, a flood of memories will accompany them.

In a home-and-home series this season and next, Texas and Arkansas will play again during the regular season. The last Razorback appearance in Austin came in 1990, when David McWilliams's Longhorns crushed Arkansas, 49–17. It was an all-too-familiar finish for a proud program which rose to great heights under Broyles, but always seemed foiled by Royal's Longhorns in the 20 years in which his teams competed against them. In fact, in the 20 meetings between Royal and Broyles, Texas won 15 and Arkansas five.

This will be the 75th meeting between the two schools in a series that began in 1894. And over the years, Texas has dominated, 54–20. That is one strong reason the rivalry in Arkansas is a whole lot more heated than it is in Texas. Of those 20, three of them came in the window in the middle of the 1960s, when Broyles's teams denied Texas a national championship in 1964 and posted back-to-back wins in 1965 and 1966. Broyles's teams won in 1960 in Austin and in 1971 in Little Rock. Otherwise, Royal's teams prevailed.

The world remembers—and if it didn't, it will be thoroughly reminded this week—the famed "Game of the Century," the Longhorns' 15–14 victory in Fayetteville, Arkansas, in 1969. That was known as "the Big Shootout," matching the nation's number one and number two teams in the final game of the year in what was the Centennial Year of college football. A year later, the game billed as "Shootout Two" resulted in a Razorback misfire, as Texas claimed its 30th-straight win and second National Championship with a 42–7 victory in Austin. But the staunch historians of Texas football, while acknowledging with the rest of the world that the James-Street-to-Randy-Peschel pass in 1969 is the most famous play in the series, would maintain it is not the most important.

For had it not been for a young sophomore named Jack Crain 30 years before, Street's heroics likely would never have been in a position to happen.

In his various definitions of the word "*renaissance,*" our friend Webster uses the words "*rebirth*" and "*revival.*"

And that is what happened in 1939 when Jack Crain touched the ball in the final minute of play against Arkansas.

D. X. Bible had been hired in 1937, at the unheard-of salary of $15,000, to rekindle the flame of Texas football. It had been flickering for a decade, and not long after Jack Chevigny's team beat Notre Dame 7–6 in 1934, it had gone out. Following seasons of 4–6 in 1935 and 2–6–1 in 1936, Chevigny was fired.

Bible, who had tremendous success at Texas A&M and Nebraska, was heralded as the savior.

But after a 2–6–1 season in 1937 and a 1–8 year in 1938, fans, who were none too pleased with his salary in the wake of the Great Depression, started calling him "Ali Bible and the Forty Sieves," a reference to what they obviously considered a leak in Bible's defensive construction.

And so it was that Texas came to the 1939 Arkansas game in Austin, having just lost to Oklahoma 24–12, and with little hope for a change.

"Things had been down for so long," says Bill Sansing, who watched the game as a student and later became the Longhorns' first sports information director. "There was a loser mentality. We were losing again, 13–7, with a minute to play. No one could have expected what was about to happen."

Many in the so-so crowd of 17,000 who had come to see if the Longhorns could win their first conference opener since 1933 were headed to the exits. Only 30 seconds remained. In the huddle, quarterback Johnny Gill gathered his teammates and changed a play, and therefore the face of Texas football.

Gill directed Crain, the halfback, to switch positions with him. He told Crain to brush block the end and drift out into the flat for a screen pass. Fullback R. B. Patrick took the ball, and he threw.

To that point, Texas had just five first downs and 78 yards of offense. Only an 82-yard quick kick return for a touchdown by Crain had put the 'Horns on the scoreboard.

Cowboy Jack Crain would become a Texas legend and go on to serve in the Texas legislature, but nothing he would ever do would have an impact on something as much as his weaving run for 67 yards and a touchdown. Only seconds remained when he crossed the south goal line, tying the score at 13, and it took several minutes to clear the fans from the field so Crain could kick what turned out to be the game-winning extra point.

Years after his Hall of Fame coaching career was over, Bible recalled the significance. "That play and that victory changed our outlook—mine, the players', the student body's, and the ex-students'," said Bible. "Things had been going pretty badly up until that game. The way was still long, but we had tasted the fruits of victory and we were on our way."

The Longhorns finished 5–4 that year, posting their first winning season in six years, but the foundation was in place. Over the next seasons, Bible would field some of the greatest teams in Texas and Southwest Conference history, and he would end his career at Texas as athletics director, a post from which he hired Darrell Royal as the Longhorns coach in December 1956. When Royal was so supportive of the hiring of Mack Brown in 1997, 60 years of Longhorn legacy had come full circle.

Sansing, the wordsmith, said it best, and he didn't even have to look the word up in Webster.

"It was the renaissance of Texas football," he said. "Before that, everything was down. After that, everything was on the way up."

Victor Davis, the *Dallas Morning News*

FIELD'S 60-YARD DASH BEATS TECH IN COTTON BOWL

The 1943 Cotton Bowl marked the Longhorns' very first bowl game. Underdogs to fifth-ranked Georgia, which had won both of its first two bowl appearances, Texas rose to the occasion, as described in the following day's Dallas Morning News.

Inspired University of Texas football stalwarts, behind a pile-driving line which performed almost perfectly over the route, rode over Georgia Tech's Yellow Jackets Friday afternoon at Cotton Bowl Stadium to win by a 14–7 count the seventh game of the annual New Year's Day gridiron classic.

It was one of the sweetest triumphs an orange-clad team has ever turned in for Skipper D. X. Bible, whose happy smile after the game stretched clear across his face and far back on the bald spot of his head. Sharing in the fruits of a well-earned Longhorn victory was a strictly partisan crowd of 36,000 deliriously joyful fans, an excellent turnout under present-day conditions.

Pretty near perfect it was—for Texas fans.

The weather was ideal, the best in the bowl's history. The crowd was tops, too. And in the football department Bible's lads roundly outplayed the conquerors of Notre Dame, Alabama, and Duke most of the way to bring a finish which found sound satisfaction for every Texan present.

Longhorn Line Performs
The story of the game was pretty simple. The big, fast, bruising Longhorn line Friday was a superb thing to watch. It cleared the way ahead for the Texas backs to plunge and gallop, and on defense, until Tech's final period outburst, kept the Ramblin' Wreck attack so well shackled the southerners were almost helpless.

Behind the magnificent performance of the white-shirted forwards, the Longhorn backs drove hard and fast. Time after time it was third down and five, and in this crucial spot the Steer ball luggers not only got the five, but often made it seven and eight.

Sheer beauty it was, if you'll pardon our rapture, to watch the Texas forwards operate. It was about as close to perfection in the way of line play as will ever be seen.

It was a colorful ball game, with thrills aplenty, and despite the fact the Wrecks were badly outplayed for three periods, they staged a last-period windup which netted one quick touchdown and had the tying marker in sight before the Longhorns dug in to hold on their 4-yard stripe.

Rather apparent from the first was the game's outcome when the opening plays showed this Texas team was primed to the gills and the line was out-handling the Tech forwards.

Texas Gets Rolling

Texas started rolling midway of the opening period after Joe Schwarting nabbed Bill McHugh's fumble on the Longhorn 48. It took 12 plays to eat up the yardage remaining from there to pay dirt. Roy McKay started it off with a pass to Wally Scott to the Tech 42, and the same combination clicked again to advance the leather to the 29. Jackie Field picked up five more at right end, added four through the middle, and McKay followed with a smash which carried to the Engineers' 14. Three line plays by McKay, Field, and Max Minor netted but eight yards. That made it fourth down and two to go on the Jacket 6. Field cracked right tackle for the yardage, and the Longhorns had four downs from the 4 to make it.

McKay got a yard of it in a drive over left guard. Then came the payoff. McKay faded back and shot a pass into the end zone. Clint Castleberry, Tech's brilliant freshman All-American back, slapped at the ball but merely deflected it into the waiting arms of Minor, who nabbed the hoghide just inches from the out-of-bounds line. He fell out of bounds after completing the catch, but the six-pointer went up on the board as the play actually was made within the end zone.

From placement, Jackie Field added the seventh point.

The Longhorns kept Tech well bottled up through the second period but were unable to launch a sustained drive themselves, and the half found Texas in front, 7–0.

Field Gallops 60 Yards

Jackie Field, the lad with the twinkling heels, sacked up the victory for Texas in the third period with the game's longest run—a beautiful 60-yard sprint through the entire Jacket 11.

It came after Tech had bogged down a Longhorn drive on the Engineers' 10-yard line. J. A. Helms, Tech wingman, stepped back to the goal line and lifted a beauty of a punt, which the Steer sprinter nabbed on his own 40. He got a perfect block by Jack Freeman to get him started, and he did the rest. Running hard and fast, he brushed off Tech tacklers and then broke into the clear. His stride wasn't broken all the way. This time McKay booted the extra point.

To the credit of the Georgians, they didn't fold. Quite to the contrary, in fact, as many a Longhorn fan got the shakes during a spirited comeback the visitors staged in the closing period.

Early in the final chapter Castleberry lugged a Texas punt back to the Georgians' 33, and from there the Engineers rolled all the way.

Striking mainly through the air, they went 67 yards for the touchdown through a Longhorn team which, at that time, was made up mainly of third-stringers.

Castleberry slipped through the line for nine, and R. W. Sheldon made it first down on the Tech 44. Then came a honey of a pass, Sheldon to J. A. Marshall, good for 32 yards and a first down on the Steer 24. In three line thrusts Castleberry netted but a couple of yards, but the Engineers kept the drive alive with a last-down toss. It read Castleberry to Helms and was good for 15 yards and a first and 10 on the Longhorn 6.

Steers Caught Napping

The Orange forwards were pretty tough about it for three plays, limiting Dodd and Prokop to two yards in three tries, but on the final down, the Georgians caught the Steers napping with one of the oldest chestnuts in the book—the Statue of Liberty play. They had tried it a couple of times before without success, but here in the clutch, David Eldridge plucked the cherry from Castleberry's hands and slanted off left end for the touchdown. Jordan's place kick was partially blocked but had enough momentum to wobble between the uprights for the extra point.

Well, Longhorn fans figured that was just a flash and settled back in their seats. But they got jumpy in a hurry when the Engineers barged right back to knock at the door again.

The stage for the second drive was set when McKay's poor punt sailed out of bounds on the Tech 46. Prokop started it off with a strike to Sheldon, which the latter caught on the Texas 42. After a line play added yardage, Prokop went back to pitching and this time connected with Marshall for 28 yards and a first down on the Texas 9. The Jackets drew a five-yard tax here, but Jordan got that back and four yards more on a triple reverse which carried to the 5.

The Texas crowd was sweating right here, brother, and not from the heat. But the Steers dug in, nailed Prokop after a yard gain, and

Sheldon's pass across the line was wild, probably because he had a swarm of Texas forwards on his neck. That left it last down and four to go for the score which could tie the game. Tech's in-the-pinch effort was feeble. Sheldon faded back to pass, but the ball somehow rolled off his hand as he aimed to fire. The play fizzled, and Texas took over.

The Longhorns took no further chances. Back again they went to the business of banging through the Georgia Tech line, and the gun found them still driving after racking up two first downs.

Field's Dash Clincher

As it turned out, Field's fleet dash in the third period was the clincher. But the modest Jackie, who has learned long ago that backs don't romp unless the boys up front are moving 'em out of the way, would be the first to give the game's accolade to the boys who earned it—that magnificent, bristling Texas line.

How completely the Orange forwards outplayed their vaunted rivals is shown by the cold figures, which didn't lie a bit in this instance. Tech, noted for a hard-driving running game, picked up but 57 yards in this manner as compared to 201 for the victors. Holding Tech to 57 yards on the ground is something that just wasn't done by any team during this regular season—not even Georgia, which handled the Jackets in their lone setback of the 1942 campaign.

Tech coaches after the game ruefully admitted they had been shown. To a man they stamped the fine Texas line as the best they had met all season—Georgia, Notre Dame, Duke, and Alabama and the rest.

Quite a compliment this to the Bible brand of football, especially in view of the fact that the tough southeastern circuit long has looked upon Southwest Conference football as a lot of silly forward-passing razzle-dazzle.

As has been remarked, it was a sweet triumph for the Texas coach. It was Texas's first venture in bowl play, and the result was not only extremely pleasing to the legion of Longhorn exes, but generally helpful to the Southwest Conference as a whole. It was a prestige ball game—Georgia Tech really rates in national football—and the Longhorns won it, not with the fabled Southwest pass-and-pray system, but with honest-to-gosh sound old fundamental football. The writer doubts if there is a team in the country which could have stopped the Texas power Friday.

So close was the Texas defense it made the flashy Castleberry, Tech's ace back, look bad at times. But nevertheless, the kid showed he had the stuff even in the face of adverse conditions. He just could go because his line couldn't budge those tough babies with Orange on 'em. And the fact Texas covered him with four men didn't help either.

Frank Guess, the Longhorn freshman kicking star, had a few minutes of glory in the second period. Operating with veterans around him, the kid looked good. He'll be scampering this fall.

Crowd Pleased Officials

Cotton Bowl officials were tickled pink at the turnout. There were few vacant spots in the big bowl, and the last-minute press for tickets was so great they were still passing them out well along in the second period.

All told, [it was] a colorful, brilliant spectacle and one of the best games the seven-year-old classic has produced. It will be a long train ride back for Atlanta for coach W. A. "Bill" Alexander's boys. This, incidentally, was their first defeat in three bowl starts.

Shirley Povich, *Washington Post*

GILMER FAILURE AS RIVAL STARS

In a highly anticipated pairing of star quarterbacks, the Longhorns' Bobby Layne got the measure of Alabama's Harry Gilmer to give Texas an easy victory in the 1948 Sugar Bowl as reported here by Shirley Povich, the legendary columnist from the Washington Post.

Blond-haired Bobby Layne was the sweetest item in the Sugar Bowl today, and before 72,000 close-packed fans, Texas University raced to a 277 victory over Alabama's frustrated football team.

Layne passed to one of Texas's four touchdowns, scrambled with the ball to another, and made high mockery of his long-awaited duel with Harry Gilmer of Alabama.

Statistics

Texas		Alabama
14	First downs	7
59	Yards gained rushing	41
24	Forward passes attempted	17
11	Forward passes completed	4
62	Yards gained forward passing	183
2	Forward passes intercepted by	0
30	Yards gained runback int. passes	0
29.3	Punting average (from scrimmage)	38.6
110	Total yards all kicks returned	121
1	Opponent fumbles recovered	2
5	Yards lost by penalties	15

Up from the obscurity of line play came three Texas substitutes to lend Layne a powerful hand with the demolition of Alabama's Sugar Bowl hopes.

On a kick blocked by tackle George Petrovich and recovered in the end zone by guard Victor Vasicek, Texas bolted out of a 7–7 tie in the third quarter and launched its rout of the Crimson Tide.

Layne, Gilmer Poles Apart

And in the fourth quarter it was another substitute, end Lewis Holder, who intercepted one of Gilmer's passes for Texas's third touchdown and, a bit later, downed a Gilmer fumble to set up the fourth.

But it was Layne, panicking 'Bama with his passes and running the ball on bootleg plays from his quarterback post in the T formation, who was the transcendent figure on a day when his supposed opposite number, Gilmer, was sadly inadequate.

Layne was the game's leading gainer even at rushing the ball.

Gilmer, rushed remorselessly by the Texas line, experienced the worst day of his career in the 'Bama backfield, completing only three of the 12 passes he threw.

Texas's big third touchdown was a Gilmer pass that boomeranged into Holder's interception, and Texas's fourth touchdown stemmed from a Gilmer fumble on the 5-yard line.

'Bama End "Steals" Score

The 'Bama line averted an even more crushing defeat for the Crimson Tide, stopping Texas's running game once on the 1-foot line, and turning back two other Texas threats inside the 10-yard line.

Even on Alabama's one scoring play, a 6-yard pass by Gilmer, the Crimson Tide quarterback was made to look good only by a sensational maneuver by his end Ed White, who virtually stole the touchdown for 'Bama.

Gilmer's pass was intercepted on the goal line by Jim Canady, Texas halfback, and wrested away from him by White in a tussle in the end zone.

The statistics show how completely Texas took charge, especially in the second half, when Alabama failed to pierce the Texas 45-yard line until the last two minutes of play.

Texas Monopolizes Ball

The figures show Texas controlled the ball for 74 plays, while Alabama had it for only 34.

Layne served notice of his passing skill the second time Texas gained the ball, connecting with three of the first four passes on a 75-yard march that consumed only 10 plays.

He pitched a 49-yarder to [Billy] Pyle on the 'Bama 17, and then ate up a seven-yard chunk with a flanker pass to Canady. From 5 yards out he found Blount in the end zone for the first touchdown.

Gilmer was a luckless guy on the final play of the first quarter when he tore off 17 yards past midfield, only to stumble and fall with blockers and a clear field ahead. He took 'Bama to the Texas 25 before missing a fourth-down pass to [Jim] Cain.

Canady Averts Shutout

A 35-yard punt return by [Monk] Moseley launched the tying touchdown for 'Bama midway in the second quarter, and [Red] Noonan breached the Texas line for important gains of eight and 12 yards before White grabbed Gilmer's touchdown pass away from Canady of Texas.

Layne's passes took Texas deep into 'Bama territory in the third quarter before Texas lost the ball, and Moseley was sent in to punt out of danger.

Out of the Texas line bolted Petrovich with amazing suddenness to smother Moseley's boot, and the ball rolled free into the end zone, where Vasicek pounced on it for the score that put Texas in front, 14–7.

Alabama never got back in the ballgame. Layne put 'em deep in their own territory, faking a handoff and then hiding the ball on his hip to scamper 35 yards to the Alabama 7.

'Bama Holds on One-Foot Line

When the 'Bama line braced, Layne attempted a placekick from the 21 that was wide. Again Layne took Texas into touchdown territory with superb passes to [Ralph] Blount and [Max Andrew] Bumgardner for 15 and 23 yards, and an offside play by 'Bama gave Texas a first down on the 'Bama 5.

The 'Bama line stopped Canady twice, and on fourth down stopped him again to take over the ball on their own one-foot line.

The game broke wide upon a bit later. Gilmer, aiming a pass at [Lowell] Tew from his own 9, was far off his mark, and the ball settled into the eager arms of Holder, who scampered like a jackrabbit down the sidelines for 25 yards and Texas's third touchdown.

Layne Goes Over

Alabama received the next kickoff, and in five plays Texas scored. Petrovich rushed Gilmer for a 10-yard loss on a passing attempt, and when Gilmer shifted to a running game, Holder hit him so hard at left end he fumbled. Holder recovered on the 'Bama 5.

Layne then snaked to the 1, but an offside penalty put Texas back on the 'Bama 9.

Layne faked a handoff and took the ball himself around right end for eight and a half yards, and on the following play, he sneaked it through center for Texas's fourth touchdown with only two minutes remaining.

Lineup and Game Summary

Texas		Alabama
Bumgardner	LE	Steiner
Harris	LT	Whitley
Magliolo	LG	Wozniak
Rowan	Center	Mancha
Fry	RG	Richeson
Kelley	RT	Flowers
Schwartzkopf	RE	Cain
Gillory	QB	Morrow
Pyle	LH	Gilmer
Canady	RH	Codenhead
Landry	FB	Tew

Score by Quarters

Texas	7	0	7	13	27
Alabama	0	7	0	0	7

Touchdowns: Texas—Blount (for Schwartzkopf). Vasicek (for Magliolo). Holder (for Bumgardner), Layne (for Gillory). Points after touchdowns—Guess (for Layne). 3 (placements). Touchdown: Alabama—White (for Steiner). Point after touchdown—Morrow (placement).

George Minot, *Washington Post*

LONGHORNS SCORE EARLY, WIN, 28-7

The October 1963 battle for supremacy at the Cotton Bowl between number one Oklahoma and number two Texas proved to be no contest as the 'Horns jumped out to an early lead and never looked back on their way to the national championship.

"We're number one, we're number one," chanted the Texas students, and before the sun had dipped below the rim of the jam-packed Cotton Bowl today their football team proved it.

By a thumping, 28-7 victory the lean, cowboy-tough Longhorns chased the Sooners of Oklahoma clear back to Norman.

The two giants of college football—Oklahoma rated number one, Texas number two—entered the steaming-hot Cotton Bowl seemingly as equals. Both were undefeated. In addition, the Sooners, the last time out, had toppled defending national champion Southern California.

But the Longhorns asserted their superiority from the opening kickoff when they drove 68 yards for a touchdown, and they never let up.

The Texas line, anchored by 239-pound tackle Scott Appleton, was far superior, opening holes on offense and refusing to be blocked out on defense.

Sooners Swarmed

The Texans pursued with speed and abandon, and swarmed like wolves over the vaunted Oklahoma running team of Jim Grisham and Joe Don Looney, allowing them no running room until the game was far out of reach.

Operating behind their panther-quick forward wall, quarterbacks Duke Carlisle and Marvin Kristynik directed the Texas team to a touchdown in each period.

Carlisle thrilled the crowd of 75,504 with his slashing cutbacks on option plays. And when the Sooners converged to stop him, he'd give delayed handoffs to the Longhorns' best runner, tailback Tommy Ford.

Complete Only One Pass

Four different men scored for Texas: Carlisle and halfback Phil Harris from close-in, Ford on a 12-yard scamper behind a swarm of blockers, and end George Sauer on a 13-yard pass from Kristynik.

It was the only completion in three passes by the Longhorns, who believe the football was invented to kick and run and a player's job is to block and tackle as hard as possible.

Not until 21 points had been rung up by the Texans did Oklahoma finally score. Reserve quarterback John Hammond, a sophomore, made the touchdown on a three-yard run with time running out in the third quarter.

For the sixth straight year, Texas coach Darrell Royal was beating his old mentor, Bud Wilkinson, and the pattern of the game was set in the first two series of downs.

Texas took the opening kickoff back to its 32 and immediately went to work. Carlisle ran to his left, cut off a tackle through a big hole, and ran for 14 yards.

Then he did the same thing on the other side of the scattered Sooners line for 15 yards.

Ford took a delayed handoff and, following a couple of blockers, made eight yards. Then he made seven. Off and running.

With the ball on Oklahoma's 2, fourth down, Carlisle ran laterally then sliced between defenders Jackie Cowan and Dave Voiles before they could close the trap. Tony Crosby, who was to run his conversion string to 16 for 16 before the afternoon was over, made it 70, and Texas was off and running.

On Oklahoma's first play from scrimmage, the Longhorns showed they had the stickier defense. End Knox Nunnally knifed in and, grabbing [Joe Don] Looney around the ankles, threw that All-American for a three-yard loss.

Only once in the first half did the outclassed Sooners penetrate inside the Texans' 45. They made it to the 34 following a poor kick by Bob Crouch, called up from the track squad earlier this week to replace injured kicking ace Ernie Koy.

But this mild threat was choked off by Texas end Pete Lammons, who intercepted a pass. Lammons also stopped the Oklahomans later when he smothered quarterback Hammond for a seven-yard loss.

After Ford followed blockers Carlisle, George Brucks, and Hal Philipp into the end zone, Washington's John Flynn got into the act.

The big end grabbed a 15-yard pass and, running from a wing position, gained six yards on an end run. But the halftime whistle closed out this mild rally.

Flynn said in the dressing room after the game that he suffered a mild concussion and didn't remember much of what went on.

Big Appleton had a ham-like hand in Texas's third score.

He forced quarterback Bobby Page into making a hasty pitchout, and when halfback Lance Rentzel fumbled the poor toss, Appleton covered the ball on OU's 18.

Ford made most of the yardage on short bursts, but they [the team] gave the touchdown honor to Harris, who won a footrace for the flag from the 3-yard line.

A 17-yard pass, Hammond to Al Bumgardner, got the Sooners booming. Then Grisham, whom Sammy Baugh has called "pro bait," finally broke loose for 14 yards.

Hammond, a sophomore from Tulsa, got the touchdown after a slick fake to Grisham.

When Larry Vermillion recovered a Texas fumble on the Longhorns' 28 on the next series of downs, the Oklahoma stands started jumping.

But on third and 7, Hammond never got a chance to look for a pass receiver. He was pinned in the burly arms of Appleton for a seven-yard loss.

Texas controlled things after that and even added a bit of salt to gaping wounds when second-stringer Kristynik flipped over the head of Sooner Virgil Boll in the last minute.

Game Summary

Texas	7	7	7	7	28
Oklahoma	0	0	7	0	7

Texas—Carlisle (3, run); Crosby (kick).
Texas—Ford (12, run); Crosby (kick).
Texas—Harris (3, run); Crosby (kick).
Oklahoma—Hammond (3, run); Jarman (kick).
Texas—Sauer (14, pass from Kristynik); Crosby (kick).
Attendance—75,514.

Statistics

	Texas	Oklahoma
First Downs	16	8
Rushing Yardage	239	127
Passing Yardage	14	63
Passes	1–3	4–10
Passes Intercepted	3	0
Punts	5–30	5–33
Fumbles Lost	1	1
Yards Penalized	39	50

Walter Robertson, *Dallas Morning News*

LONGHORNS EXPLODE NAVY MYTH, 28-6

Heisman Trophy winner Roger Staubach and his Navy team were the final obstacle facing the Longhorns as they went about wrapping up their first national championship in the Cotton Bowl on New Year's Day in 1964.

It already had been crowned king of the 1963 college football season, but a magnificent University of Texas team chose New Year's Day 1964 to brandish its crown before the football world and a good but bewildered Navy opponent.

The score was Texas 28, Navy 6 in this 28th Cotton Bowl Classic that had been billed as possibly the bowl "dream" match of all time.

Indeed, it turned out to be just that. For few among the packed Cotton Bowl house of 75,504 or the millions of viewers who made up possibly the largest television audience in college football history dreamed it would happen the way it did on a crisp, bright, blue afternoon.

The staggering, sometimes chilling efficiency with which the Texas defense ended the legend of a Navy offense based on Heisman Trophy winner Roger Staubach's scrambling tactics might have been suspicioned in the depths of a prolific imagination.

But to have predicted that 28 Texas points would be fashioned principally on passing would have invited a sanity examination.

Nonetheless, it was the stunning air game which Longhorn quarterback Duke Carlisle flaunted before his disbelieving audience, combined with a brutal Steer defense, that forged this victory which must stand as one of the most prominent ever achieved by a Southwest Conference football team.

Carlisle, who late was given an overwhelming vote by writers as the game's outstanding back, completed seven of 19 passes for 213 yards and two touchdowns.

Those two touchdowns came on long-range missiles, almost unheard of in the Longhorn arsenal, and both were to wingback Phil

Harris, for 58 yards before the game was three minutes old and for 63 yards less than midway of the second quarter.

And then, virtually to seal the amazing victory before the expected battle to the death was half over, Carlisle waltzed nine yards on a splendidly executed roll-out option for the third Texas touchdown with 2:39 remaining in the second period.

After seeing one 80-yard march fizzle on Tony Crosby's missed field-goal attempt from the 12-yard line midway of the third quarter, the Longhorns ran the count to 28–0 with 2:40 left in the third when fullback Harold Philipp slammed across from the 2.

But it was another pass, a 21-yarder to soph George Sauer from Tommy Wade, the man who was supposed to be the passing specialist in Texas's renowned ground-power attack, that set up the score at the Navy 5.

Texas was deprived a fifth touchdown by a matter of inches and a racing clock. With reserves deep from the bench in the game for the chance at some shavings of the glory, Texas ripped to the Navy 6-inch line, largely on three huge smashes by Tom Stockton. But a desperation lunge on fourth down by Hix Green was barely short as time ran out.

It was not until the early moments of the final quarter that Navy finally pushed 74 yards to put its six points on the scoreboard.

And it was not until Staubach abandoned his scrambling tactics to rely on his marvelous throwing arm that the Middies were able to do that.

Staubach passed for 57 of those yards and scored the touchdown himself on a roll-out option from the 2.

Obviously, it was much too late for Navy, the champions of the East who had pledged themselves to prove their dynasty should be the college football world.

Roger, Ref Flee for Life

But those dreams of supremacy by the Middies were crushed before the first quarter was half gone, crushed beneath the grinding muscle of Steer ends Knox Nunnally and Pete Lammons as they nearly rushed Staubach and a fleeing official from the very stadium.

Navy had just intercepted a Carlisle pass on its own 40, and on first down Staubach turned to retreat, scatter the enemy defenses in his favorite fashion, and then strike terror in their hearts with his usually incredible escape tactics. But he didn't even have time to glance over his shoulder to see where the thunder of stampeding feet was coming from.

Neither did referee David Buchanan of Scarsdale, New York. He leaped for his life from the path just before Nunnally and Lammons buried Staubach for a 22-yard loss.

This play is important in the scheme of things that were to come only in that it set the pattern of the first half in which that furious Texas rush and Carlisle's surprising pass offensive stashed away victory.

Time after bruising time All-American tackle Scott Appleton, who was to be chosen the game's outstanding lineman by a wide margin, guard George Brucks, linebacker Tom Nobis, ends [Ben] House, Nunnally and Charles Talbert, or any number of orange-shirted demons, would flood through to thwart Staubach at every turn.

In the second half, Staubach contented himself with dropping straight back and firing quickly, obviously the only way the Middies were to be able to move against the furious challenge of the Texas defense.

Carlisle Owned the Record Briefly

It was too late for the good judgment to overcome the Longhorns. But it was in time for Staubach to write his name in the Cotton Bowl record book. He finished the day with 21 completions in 31 passing attempts for 228 yards, both record-setting performances.

But Staubach lost 47 yards fleeing for his life while attempting those first-half throws, allowing Carlisle to emerge as the new record holder for total offense in a Cotton Bowl game with 267 yards—213 passing and 54 rushing.

In fact, Carlisle briefly also owned the passing yardage record. He retired from the game late in the third quarter, completely unworried about such trivial things as individual records. For Duke and the 'Horns he had directed so masterfully through the grand, 11-victory season, long before they had accomplished what they determinedly set out to do.

Had not Carlisle grabbed such a huge share of the glory in this one for Texas, a number-one hero candidate might well have been Harris, the sophomore wingback from San Antonio. He made a great fake to leave Navy safetyman Robert Sutton lying helplessly on his face on his first touchdown catch from Carlisle. And he made a great catch on the second one after Middie defender Pat Donnelly slapped the ball and even appeared for a moment to have intercepted it. But Harris clutched it to his chest at the Navy 35, got a clearing block from Talbert at the 25, and romped across untouched.

Ironically, the final score was virtually the same as that by which Texas defeated Oklahoma on this same Cotton Bowl field the afternoon of October 12 to become claimant to the title of the nation's number-one team.

That was the day the fabled story of perhaps the finest football team the Southwest Conference ever has known really began. But New Year's Day 1964 is the one that will perpetuate it.

Robert Markus, *Chicago Tribune*

TEXAS RALLIES TO BEAT ARKANSAS, 15–14

With President Nixon on hand to award the national championship to the victor, the top-ranked Longhorns fell behind second-ranked Arkansas by two touchdowns before rallying for one of their most unforgettable triumphs.

Frank Broyles, the Arkansas coach, said all week that Texas's Darrell Royal had a loaded Derringer in his hip pocket. Today Royal's Longhorns waited until the final 5 minutes to pull the trigger, but when they did, it was lethal.

The weapon Broyles was referring to was Texas's seldom-used passing attack. The Longhorns completed only six passes all day today, but the last one, on what surely was the most audacious call in college football history, turned a budding upset into a 15–14 Texas triumph over Arkansas in a stirring and dramatic confrontation of unbeaten football powers.

The situation was this: Arkansas was leading Texas 14–8 with four minutes, 47 seconds remaining in the game. Texas had fourth down and three on its own 43. Many of the 44,000 fans packed into Razorback stadium expected Texas to punt. Those who did not expected a running play, probably off the famed triple option. Nobody expected what happened.

Quarterback James Street faked a handoff to fullback Steve Worster, raced back into the pocket, and arched a bomb far upfield. Tight end Randy Peschel, the only receiver out, ran under it at the Arkansas 13, where he was showed out of bounds.

Two plays later, halfback Jim Bertelsen lunged over left guard two yards for the touchdown, and Happy Feller kicked the point that sent Texas soaring to the national championship.

It also sent the Longhorns into the Cotton Bowl on New Year's Day to play Notre Dame. Arkansas, which played brilliantly while suffering its only loss of the season, goes to the Sugar Bowl to face Mississippi.

Seldom has a sporting event so completely fulfilled all expectations as this one did. The residents of this little community in the Ozarks have talked about nothing but this football game all week. It was a battle between the top two teams in the country to decide the Southwest Conference and national championships.

Everybody expected a classic battle—and they got it.

The largest crowd ever to attend a game in Razorback Stadium—President Nixon among them—saw Arkansas carry a 14–0 lead into the final period.

Then, on the first play of the quarter, Street ran 42 yards on a broken play for a touchdown. Never hesitating a moment, the quarterback called his own number again, sprinted out to the left, and knifed over for the two extra points that cut Arkansas's lead to 14–8.

Arkansas, which according to Street, defensed Texas's dreadnought attack "better than anybody all year," had the Longhorns on the ropes when they forced them to their fourth-down decision.

Wasn't Going to Kick

Royal said he never considered punting the football. "I figured if we kicked the ball, there wouldn't be but a few minutes left when we got it back, and we need longer to operate than that. Even if we'd just run for the first down, we'd have needed all the time we had left."

Royal called Street to the sidelines, and they discussed the possibilities. Said Street: "We'd been running the option play all day. It's our strength, and we felt they'd feel we'd be running it. They'd been supporting real fast with their defensive backs."

Peschel said he was not surprised when he heard Street call the play in the huddle. "Jim said to me, 'Randy, you know that's to you. If you get behind him, run like hell. Otherwise, get the first down.' I had an option on the play. If the halfback stayed with me, I could break in front of him and pick up the first down, but I got a step on him. But, I'm not too fast, and he caught up to me and the safety came over and both had a shot at the ball."

It Finally Worked

The play, explained Peschel, is called 53 veer pass, and "we've run it three or four times this year. This is the first time we completed it."

Street, at least in his own mind, had an option, too: "As I went back into the pocket, it was in my mind that if he was covered well I would run with it. I wasn't going to throw the ball away.

"Then I saw him get a step on the defensive back. Peschel made the greatest catch there ever was, I guess. I couldn't see him catch it. All I saw was the referee throw his arms up to signal catch, and oh boy, was I happy. I knew then we'd go in to score."

Ted Koy cracked 11 yards over left tackle on the play before Bertelsen scored. When Feller kicked Texas into the lead, Arkansas still had nearly four minutes to come back.

And the way Bill Montgomery had been throwing and Chuck Dicus catching, nobody doubted that it was possible. Dicus had caught one touchdown pass from Montgomery and had another one called back because of a penalty. Before the game was over, he [Dicus] was to slip into the seams of the Texas defense for nine receptions and 146 yards.

But on this advance, Montgomery turned to his tailback, Bobby Burnett, as his primary receiver. He threw to him three times in a drive that moved the Razorbacks from their 20 to the Texas 39.

Then, with just 1:13 left in the game, [Montgomery] aimed a pass to flanker John Rees at the sideline. Texas's Tom Campbell intercepted, and Texas had prevailed.

But what a struggle it was for the nation's number-one team. President Nixon's helicopter had just landed in the practice field outside the stadium when a great roar went up from the crowd. If the president thought it was for him, he was mistaken.

Sparkling Catch

It was the reaction to the first big break of the game, Koy's fumble on Texas's second play from scrimmage.

Arkansas recovered at the Longhorn 22, and the president managed to get to his seat in time to see Burnett dive over a pile from the 1 to score the touchdown.

It was set up by a great catch by Rees at the 2 on a third-down play. When Bill McClard kicked the extra point, it was 7–0, and scarcely more than a minute and a half had been played.

At halftime it was still that way, although Dicus had hauled in a 26-yard pass from Montgomery for an apparent touchdown that was called back.

It was the first time this year Texas had trailed at the half and, when Cotton Speyrer fumbled the second-half kickoff, the Razorback fanatics were sure another quick score was in prospect.

Not so. The Longhorns held this time, but then Speyrer fumbled again after catching a pass, and Arkansas recovered at its 47. In all, Texas was to fumble the ball away four times and throw two interceptions.

This time, Arkansas needed only five plays to boom its lead to 14–0. One of the biggest was a scrambling 18-yard run by Montgomery on third down when he was trapped trying to pass.

Then from the Texas 29 he connected with Dicus, slanting across the middle at the 10. Rees wiped out a defender with a fine block, and Dicus skipped into the end zone.

Now Texas appeared ready to crack. Street threw the ball into a crowd and was intercepted and, before you could yell, "Woooooie pig, sooie," the Razorbacks were headed for another touchdown.

But the Longhorns finally stiffened and threw Montgomery back to their 42. Then, with only 18½ minutes left in the game, Texas got the ball on its 20, trailing 14–0, its championship dreams fading into the Ozark hills.

This time, Texas did not panic. Street kept the ball on the ground and by the end of the quarter had worked it to the Arkansas 42.

Street called a pass to Peschel on the first play of the final quarter.

"I dropped to my right and felt pressure from the left," Street later recalled. "Peschel was not open, so I moved to the left and started running." He did not stop until he had covered the entire 42 yards.

Now Texas trailed 14–6 and had a decision to make. Well, not really. As Street explained later: "I rode out on the bus with Coach Royal, and he told me it had already been decided what play we'd use if we needed two points. I faked one way and came back with the option the other way. Peschel made a great block. It was the key block on the play."

Royal confirmed that the decision to use the option play for the two-pointer had been made "at 1:00 this morning when we coaches all got together and discussed it."

The two-pointer successful, Texas only trailed by six points, and the 5,000 Longhorn fans began to take hope. But Montgomery soon had them in despair.

Arkansas on the Move

Getting fantastic protection from his pass blockers and threading the ball through the Texas defense with devastating effect, Montgomery moved the Razorbacks all the way to the Texas 9. He completed passes of 20 and 21 yards to Dicus, and the second completion came immediately after an 18-yard pass to Dicus had been erased by a penalty.

Then he hit Rees for 13 more and might have had a touchdown throw to Dicus except Texas held the talented junior receiver and was penalized to its 9.

Then, on third down at the 7 and needing only a field goal to virtually insure the victory, Montgomery went to the pass once too often. He threw for Dicus in the end zone, but Danny Lester intercepted and ran it back to the 20.

Running back over the big plays later, Royal wouldn't single out one as the biggest, but said of that play: "Lester intercepted and we were out of it. A field goal there eliminates us. But there were so many big plays. Street's run, his run for two points, Campbell's interception, Feller kicking the extra point."

That's why Texas is national champion today. It made the big plays when it counted. It did not quit when defeat seemed imminent.

Walter Robertson, the *Dallas Morning News*

COMEBACK LONGHORNS DO IT AGAIN

Texas was called upon to repeat its come-from-behind heroics from the epic Arkansas game in order to overcome Joe Theismann and Notre Dame in the 1970 Cotton Bowl to seal its claim as the nation's top team.

It took college football 100 years to build up the sort of pressure that would cook a team alive. And the Texas Longhorns have to climb out of that double-boiler twice in less than four weeks to secure the 1969 season's national championship.

The Longhorns did it before an overflow crowd of 73,000 and millions of television viewers on New Year's Day, putting down a pulsating Notre Dame challenge, 21–17, in what has to be the most magnificent game of the 34-year-old Cotton Bowl Classic.

In fact, if it didn't replace Texas's dramatic 15–14 victory over Arkansas on December 6 as the all-time classic game of college football's first 100 years, it is only because the stakes weren't quite so high.

The immediate temptation would be to rank the Texas-Arkansas match as tops for the first 100 and start the second centennial running with this one.

Certainly the drama and intensity Thursday was a dead ringer for the December 6 match between number-one Texas and number-two Arkansas as Texas stormed from behind in the final period to crush the marvelous bid of a Notre Dame team making its first bowl appearance since the famed "Four Horsemen" led the Irish to victory in the Rose Bowl game exactly 45 years ago.

The three living members of the "Horsemen," in fact, sat in a 50-yard-line box Thursday to watch the superb challenge of their alma mater, led by a wisp of a quarterback about the size of the man who quarterbacked that 1925 Rose Bowl team, the late Harry Stuhldreyer.

Joe Theismann, a thin 170-pound junior from New Jersey, completed 17 of 27 passes for 231 yards, passed for two touchdowns, and drove the Steer defense frantic much of the afternoon. Even as Arkansas junior Bill Montgomery had done at Fayetteville, Arkansas, barely more than three weeks before.

And just like at Fayetteville, it was Texas's senior clutch artist, Longview [High School] quarterback James Street, who stripped all real meaning from those rival heroics.

Street was the architect of all three masterpiece touchdown drives that forged this 20th-consecutive Texas victory and the 500th in school history.

The drives covered 74, 77, and 78 yards. The first finally got Texas on the scoreboard in the first quarter, when the 10–0 Notre Dame lead looked to be the makings of the season's most colossal upset.

But it was the final two which rushed the Steers from behind both times in the final frenzied quarter and must forever stand alongside those dramatic fourth-quarter moments of the Arkansas game as cornerstones of this national championship year for Darrell Royal's team.

And, irony of ironies, it was again a last-ditch interception by defensive back Tom Campbell which cemented the victory. Campbell's sure hands clutched victory from the deep Cotton Bowl shadows as he stole a Theismann pass, perhaps the only poor one the Irish quarterback threw all afternoon, with just 29 ticks left on the scoreboard clock. Against Arkansas, Campbell had intercepted a Montgomery pass to kill a similar last-gasp effort by the Razorbacks with barely more than a minute to play.

Campbell's interception finally drained the life from a fourth quarter that defies description.

There was just a minute and two seconds to play when Theismann, undaunted by the touchdown Billy Dale had just rammed across to put Texas ahead with 1:08 to play, went to work. He has been similarly undaunted early in the period when Ted Koy circled left end untouched from the Irish 4 to give Texas a 14–10 lead.

Texas had used a whopping eight minutes and 10 seconds of the clock to fashion that go-ahead score. But it had taken Theismann only 2:56 and eight plays to get it back on an 80-yard drive that see-sawed Notre Dame back out front, 17–14.

Now, after Theismann had hit passes of 16 and 27 yards to move the Irish from their own 23 to the Texas 39, Notre Dame called its second straight timeout to stop the clock with just 38 seconds left. And when tight end Dewey Poskon circled back between two Texas defenders to stand awaiting Theismann's throw at the 18, there was no reason to believe the slight Irish magician wouldn't fire the ball right to his chest. He had done it all day, scrambling unbelievably to elude the air-grabbing pass rush most of the time.

But the ball nose lifted a bit on Theismann in this final crucial throw. It rifled above Poskon's leap by a scant few inches.

And there was Campbell, moving to the stray football like a Nike missile, to end the finest battle ever seen in the 34 years of this classic on the Cotton Bowl's muddy, battered turf.

Notre Dame, a seven-and-a-half-point underdog despite a fine 8–11 regular-season record, had staked its hopes of stopping Texas's vaunted wishbone-T attack, the Southwest Conference's most prolific in history, on the size of its four huge down linemen and the quickness of its four-linebacker squad led by Bob Olson, a demon sophomore from Superior, Wisconsin. There certainly was substance to those hopes. Notre Dame had yielded an average of only 85 yards per game during the regular season and had ranked as the nation's fourth best defensive team overall.

And the theory and hope glowed brightly for more than a quarter. Olson, who was to make a runaway of the most valuable defensive performer, ranged as swiftly and deadly as had Arkansas's linebacker Cliff Powell to slow the usually overwhelming power of Texas's full-house backfield of Street, halfbacks Ted Koy and Jim Bertelsen, and fullback Steve Worster. Olson and All-American tackle Mike McCoy paced the execution which shut down Texas's inside yardage well in the early going. The Steers managed only two first downs their first three possessions.

But Street directed the attack outside on the terrifying options and pitches to Bertelsen to open things up, especially at the vulnerable Irish left flank. And it worked to perfection. Despite the slow start, Texas rushed for a gaudy 331 yards, 155 of them by Worster, who polled 59 votes as the game's outstanding offensive hand, compared to 32 for Street and 15 for Theismann.

Certainly it was one of the greatest afternoons for Worster, the 208-pound junior from Bridge City, Texas. He slashed inside the Notre Dame ends time and again as Street's fakes of the pitchout found consistent cracks of daylight just inside the flanks.

Yet it was some of Street's finest passing of two solid seasons at the Steer helm, and his continued sleight of hand with the football which played as great a role in this classic victory for Texas.

Street completed six of 11 passes for 107 yards. And two of them, perfect strikes for 17 yards each on which Cotton Speyrer and Randy Peschel made perfect catches, igniting Texas's first touchdown thrust, which came with 11:12 left in the second period. Peschel, who made the game-saving fourth-down catch which played a leading role in the win over Arkansas, grabbed his at the Irish 27. Bertelsen then made it three straight 17-yard gainers as Koy cleared him with the type of blocking Texas's amazing running backs were throwing for each other all day. Bertelsen got the TD from the 1.

It was an incredible fake to Bertelsen ripping up the middle to be hit by at least five defenders which allowed Koy to escape untouched around left end from the 4 for the score that put Texas ahead, 14–10, early in the final period.

But the final and what proved the winning touchdown drive must be ranked as a classic of classics. The Steers had just six minutes, 47 seconds to pull it off. Enough time, of course, if they didn't lose their cool.

The Longhorns didn't. They drilled the 76 yards on 17 plays and left the bare minutes of course for the Irish to make a last stab. And again, it was a tremendous clutch play which saved it. One fourth-and-two from the Irish 10, Street had to hurry a throw under much duress. The ball was a little short for Speyrer, but the junior gamebreaker of so many an Orange afternoon twisted away from his shadowing defender, Clarence Ellis, to somehow dive under the ball before it hit the ground for a first down at the 2. Dale got the touchdown three plays later.

Theismann, who set both Cotton Bowl game passing and total offense records, guided the Irish 72 yards the first time they owned the ball but had to settle for Scott Hempel's 26-yard field goal. Then he ran the count to 10–0 on the first Irish play of the second period, arching a perfect strike to split end Tom Gatewood, who had raced well behind Texas defensive back Danny Lester.

But Lester saved face greatly with a diving interception from the hands of fullback Andy Huff at the Texas 13 to kill a spirited Irish drive late in the second quarter.

The 25 first downs each team forged were Cotton Bowl records. Texas out-totaled Notre Dame only 18 yards on offense. And even the controversial plays were about even. Notre Dame growled quite a bit about field judge Theron Thomsen's ruling that Texas had called timeout before the ball was snapped on a play which ended up with the Irish recovering a Street fumble just before the first half ended.

But Steer loyalists growled as loudly when Thomsen ruled Bertelsen and Dale were a bit short on three straight near-misses for a first down at the Notre Dame 6-yard line midway in the second quarter.

So Texas pulled it out and presented the game ball to Freddie Steinmark, the Steer safety who lost a leg to cancer a week after the Arkansas game and who watched it all on crutches on the sidelines.

Former president Lyndon Johnson was in the stands and visited both dressing rooms after the game. Richard Nixon was in the stands this time, as he [had been] at the Texas-Arkansas game, after which he personally proclaimed Texas number one, touching off secession proceedings in Pennsylvania.

The president did telephone Royal in the Steer dressing room. But this time he kept his neck snugly at his shoulders. Penn State hadn't yet gone to bat against Missouri in the Orange Bowl.

And besides, a man doesn't get to be president without enough smarts to know the risks of a foot twice exposed to a hasty mouth.

Barry Horn, *Dallas Morning News*

TEXAS WINS COTTON BOWL, 14–12

Texas won another thrilling Cotton Bowl victory in 1982 by defeating Bear Bryant's Alabama Crimson Tide to finish second in the final national rankings.

It took some time—three full quarters and almost five minutes into the fourth. It took some extra thinking—a quick timeout with one tick remaining on the 25-second play clock. It took a call that the chagrined, most valuable defensive player of the game later termed "brilliant"—a quarterback draw.

But the University of Texas Longhorns finally found their way into the Alabama end zone with 10:22 remaining in Friday's Cotton Bowl. And once they learned there indeed was a way through the Crimson Tide defense, it took the Longhorns just over eight minutes to find their way again.

And when the game ended two minutes and five seconds later, Texas was the 1982 Cotton Bowl champion, 14–12 victors over Bear Bryant's Alabama team before 73,243 spectators.

"They just whipped us in the fourth quarter," said Alabama coach Bear Bryant, who is now 1–7–1 against Texas and 314–74–16 against the rest of the world in his college coaching career.

Texas, ranked sixth, finished 10–1–1. Alabama, cochampion of the Southeastern Conference with Georgia and ranked third, dropped to 9–2–1. Alabama has never beaten Texas. The Longhorns are 7–0–1 against the Tide. Bryant's only victory over Texas came when he was at Texas A&M.

"I think this game shows why you play four quarters of football," said Texas coach Fred Akers. "In the last quarter we got better position, and our defense wasn't allowing the big play."

Alabama scored the only touchdown of the first half midway through the second quarter when quarterback Walter Lewis scrambled out of the grasp of blitzing safety Bobby Johnson and threw a six-yard touchdown to Jesse Bendross. Peter Kim kicked the extra point and added a 24-yard field goal 2:33 into the fourth quarter, and the Rolling Tide led, 10–0.

Akers and his Longhorns were still waiting for their big play. The Longhorns took Terry Sanders's kickoff after Kim's field goal, moved 30 yards until the offense, as it had done all game, bogged down—this time on the Alabama 30.

In the huddle, quarterback Robert Brewer called a sprint-out pass over the middle to Donnie Little. At the line, however, after seeing the defensive alignment, Brewer had second thoughts. With one second to get the play off or be called for delay of game, Brewer called timeout.

Quarterback Robert Brewer scored on a 30-yard run to start the Texas comeback.

"If we ran the play I had called there would have been a sack for sure from their outside pressure," said Brewer, who should have known. He was sacked seven times by the Tide defense.

"I thought it was a great call," Brewer said. "They were very surprised. I called the draw, and by the second step it went completely open. The only worry I had was if I could get my slow butt in there."

Brewer did. Raul Allegre kicked the extra point, and Texas trailed, 10–7.

"We had a full blitz on," said Alabama linebacker Robbie Jones, voted the game's most valuable defensive player. "The call was brilliant. The play was perfect for what we were in."

Still, Texas trailed by three. The Longhorns got the ball back 80 yards from the Alabama goal line with 5:59 remaining. But Brewer's passes to Little and Herkie Walls fell incomplete.

On third and 10, Brewer, who completed 12 of 21 passes for 201 yards and was named the game's most valuable offensive player, hit tight end Lawrence Sampleton with a 37-yard pass to the Alabama 43. It was Sampleton's first catch of the day.

Five plays later, Brewer and Sampleton hooked up again, this time for 19 yards to the Crimson Tide 18. A 10-yard pass to Little put the ball on the eight.

One play later, Terry Orr, the Longhorns' third-string fullback, went off tackle and found the end zone from eight yards for his first touchdown this season. Allegre kicked the extra point, and Texas, for the first time, led 14–10.

With just over two minutes remaining, Joey Jones, the Tide's kickoff return specialist, gave Alabama excellent field position for its final push. Jones took Allegre's kick on the 1 and returned it 61 yards to the Texas 38.

Alabama's Lewis tried to put the Tide up one play later. But his pass, intended for Tim Clark, was picked off by the free safety William

Graham on the 1-yard line. He was tackled immediately. He was 99 yards from the Alabama end zone. But more importantly, Alabama was one yard from the Texas goal line.

Three Brewer sneaks pushed the ball to the 4-yard line. A two-yard penalty for delay of game moved the ball back to the 2 with 56 seconds remaining. Alabama would get its chance.

Punter John Goodson took the snap one foot from the back line of the end zone and did an eight-second, one-shoed dance before he stepped out of the end zone for a safety.

"We didn't have to think very hard," said Akers. "We wanted the safety. We wanted the chance to move them as far away from the end zone as we could."

After Goodson's free kick and a 17-yard return by Jeremiah Castille, the Tide, with no timeouts left, got the ball back on their 41.

But defensive end Kiki DeAyala dropped Lewis for an eight-yard loss. Lewis picked up seven yards on the next play but could not make it out of bounds to stop the clock, and the Longhorns had their victory.

Bill Little, *Stadium Stories: Texas Longhorns*

FOURTH-AND-INCHES

After the Southwest Conference dissolved, Texas found itself a three-touchdown underdog against Nebraska in the very first Big 12 championship game in 1996. In his book, Stadium Stories, *Bill Little documented the events leading up to and culminating in one of the Longhorns' most satisfying victories.*

As he came to the line of scrimmage and surveyed the Nebraska defense in the first-ever Big 12 championship game, James Brown stood at the edge of history. Or maybe, better said, he was right smack in the middle of it. To understand the moment, it helps to understand the situation.

Our story begins long before that December afternoon, 1996, in the Trans World Dome in St. Louis. Less than three years before, there was no league championship game because there was no league. Texas was the linchpin of the Southwest Conference, and Nebraska had become the dominant team in the Big 8. But the college football world had been undergoing a metamorphosis that had actually begun in the summer of 1984.

That was when a lawsuit concerning television rights and who owned them was settled. For years, the NCAA had controlled broadcast television rights for its schools and had distributed appearances and money as it chose. As new networks emerged with interest in covering sports, the parent organization held fast to its right to control the medium. But its member institutions, particularly the leading football powers, saw a new opportunity for both money and exposure. The Universities of Georgia and Oklahoma led the way in a lawsuit, and when the court's landmark decision sided with them, it became open season in the television market.

ESPN was a new player in the arena, but it had been limited to showing games on a delayed basis while the NCAA apportioned games to its over-the-air network partners. When the Georgia-Oklahoma decision came down, ESPN quickly began seizing properties that brought nationwide exposure to programs such as Florida State and Miami, which heretofore had limited reach.

The College Football Association emerged as the steward of the television rights for the large conferences and independent universities, and that system worked until the University of Notre Dame saw an opportunity and grabbed it. The Irish signed an exclusive contract with NBC, thus breaking the CFA's control of college football weekend air time. Still, the CFA continued with a good coalition of conferences, so the issue was manageable.

But the restlessness and the positioning created a flowing stream that was not going to be denied. The dominoes began to fall in the late 1980s, and shortly after Penn State elected to join the Big Ten Conference, the musical chairs were activated.

In Austin, DeLoss Dodds was in his first decade as Texas athletics director, and he was recognized as one of the cutting-edge athletic directors in the business.

Since coming to Texas in 1981, he had watched the defection of high school recruits from Texas to other high-profile schools around the country. Attendance at league games at Houston, Rice, SMU, TCU, and Baylor had diminished tremendously despite relative success on the field. When Andre Ware won the Heisman Trophy at Houston, the Cougars averaged only 28,000 fans at their home games in the Astrodome. Part of all of that, Dodds had seen, came from the turmoil caused by recruiting scandals in the Southwest Conference. But he also knew the most important figure of all: as television was becoming such a powerful force financially and exposure-wise, the area covered by teams in the Southwest Conference had only 7 percent of America's TV sets. The Big Ten had 30 percent, even without Penn State. The Southeastern Conference had 23 percent. And the Big 8, which had even lost its regional TV package, had 7 percent.

As the dollars and the exposure opportunities began to be distributed, it was clear that the SWC and the Big 8 were in trouble.

"It usually takes a crisis to cause change," Dodds would say later, and the crisis came in the summer of 1990 when Arkansas announced it was leaving the SWC for the SEC. Rumors flew that Texas and Texas A&M were right behind the Razorbacks. But when folks go shopping, they often visit more than one store, and suddenly, the schools of the Southwest Conference were shopping or, in a couple of specific cases, being shopped.

While the old guard of the SWC entertained the notion of raiding its neighbor to the north—the Big 8—the progressives were imagining what it would be like for Texas and A&M to play Alabama and Tennessee. There was even a small but powerful group that wanted to see the Longhorns as part of the Pac 10. Conversations were held between Texas and Texas Tech (which was the closest geographically) with the Pac 10. Some even considered the possibility of Texas and

Texas A&M going their separate ways in different leagues, but that idea quickly was dispatched as nonproductive.

Before the flame could burn in either direction—west toward the Pac 10 or east toward the SEC—politics entered the picture. The state legislature and offices even as high as the governor's and lieutenant governor's squashed the idea out of deference to the Texas schools in the SWC that would be left behind.

Discussions of expanding the SWC included in-state schools such as North Texas and schools as far away as Louisville and as close as Tulane to the east. To the west, informal discussions included Brigham Young, which was part of the Western Athletic Conference.

The people in the Southwest Conference office made overtures to the Big 8 to form a television alliance, where the two leagues would remain intact but would negotiate a television package together. There was talk of a merger combining all of the schools, with a playoff game between the two league champs.

Dodds, however, looked beyond the money. His goal had always been to keep Texas in a position to compete for national honors in every sport. The Southwest Conference, an institution in college athletics for more than 75 years, was dying a slow death. Attendance was down just about everywhere except Texas and Texas A&M, and in the major sports of football and basketball, recruiting was getting harder and harder. Other schools regularly raided the football-rich arena of Texas high schools, and convincing an outstanding basketball recruit to even visit was harder and harder work.

In the Big 8, things were not a lot better. Despite the fact that both Oklahoma and Kansas had Final Four–caliber basketball programs and Missouri had a nationally respected hoops program, football was still the main attraction for television, and fact was, not many folks were being attracted.

In Texas three cities ranked among the nation's top 10 in population —Houston, Dallas, and San Antonio—and the television markets in Houston and Dallas-Fort Worth were in the top 10 television markets in the country. Denver, Kansas City, and St. Louis were the only cities in the Big 8 with any significant media markets at all. While the Southwest Conference had what was called a "regional" TV package that aired its league games over stations in the area, the Big 8 had not been able to generate one at all.

So when Dodds and Oklahoma athletics director Donnie Duncan got together to survey the landscape, they saw a far different future than those who wanted to hang on to what was.

In early 1994 the home of cards fell. The Southeastern Conference, which had added South Carolina along with Arkansas when Texas and Texas A&M chose not to leave the SWC, signed a five-year, $85 million contract with CBS. The network also signed one with the Big East for $50 million, effectively ending the CFA. The final crisis was at hand.

In the space of less than two months, the league that had begun as the Southwest Athletic Conference in 1915 was dismantled. Television negotiations pairing the Big 8 and SWC were virtually an afterthought for the networks, who were after new material. They found it when the Big 8 voted to invite Texas and Texas A&M and, with significant encouragement from Governor Ann Richards and Lieutenant Governor Bob Bullock, their respective alma maters of Baylor and Texas Tech.

Left behind were TCU, SMU, Rice, and Houston.

Texas agreed to join the merger on February 25, 1994, and on March 10, the league negotiated a television package worth $97.5 million, the most lucrative in college football history at the time, surpassing the one the SEC had cut just a month before.

The conference began play two years later, electing to split into two divisions. The North Division was exclusively former Big 8 schools, with Nebraska, Kansas, Kansas State, Iowa State, Missouri, and Colorado. In the South Division were the four former Southwest Conference schools, as well as Oklahoma and Oklahoma State. And despite opposition from the coaches at all Big 12 schools, their presidents voted to have a championship game matching the division winners and sold the package to ABC-TV.

That is how James Brown came to stand with his team on the field of the TWA Dome, with fewer than three minutes remaining and Texas nursing an improbable lead of 30–27.

Since the league's formation, the South Division had been viewed as simply cannon fodder for the powerful North Division. There was open resentment among some media, fans, and officials in the old Big 8 toward the interlopers from the four Texas schools. So it was with a degree of irony that Texas and Nebraska, two of the winningest programs in college football, would be the first representatives of the divisions to meet to decide the first-ever championship.

Nebraska, which, along with Florida State, would be the most dominant team in college football in the 1990s, was 10–1 and within striking distance of playing for a national championship. All the number-three-ranked Cornhuskers had to do was eliminate the Longhorns, which were 21-point underdogs after winning the South Division with a 7–4 overall record.

James Brown had been a significant figure in Longhorn football. He had emerged as a hero when he got his first start and beat Oklahoma, 17–10, as a redshirt freshman in 1994. He went on to lead the Longhorns to a Sun Bowl victory that season, becoming the first African American quarterback at Texas to start and win a bowl game.

In that 1994 season, a year that was tenuous at best for Coach John Mackovic, it was Brown who effectively turned the year—and Mackovic's tenure at Texas—around as he led UT to a 48–13 win over Houston and a 63–35 victory over Baylor.

In 1995 [Mackovic] had piloted Texas to the final Southwest Conference championship, including a gutsy performance despite a severe ankle sprain in a 16–6 victory over Texas A&M in the league's last game ever. In leading Texas to a 10–11 record, he helped the Longhorns earn an appearance in the Bowl Alliance in the Sugar Bowl.

The Monday before the Nebraska game, Brown had walked into a press conference in Austin and stunned the media. Badgered by a reporter about the fact that Texas was a 21-point underdog, and "How do you feel about that?" Brown finally responded, "I don't know…we might win by 21 points."

In fewer than five minutes, it was on the national wire: "Brown Predicts Texas Victory."

Mackovic, who was in his fifth season at Texas, told his quarterback in a meeting that afternoon, "Now that you've said it, you'd better be ready to back it up."

The TWA Dome was packed, with a decidedly Nebraska flavor for the game that would decide the first Big 12 championship. James Brown had led his team on the field in warm-ups and was out-cheering the cheerleaders in the pregame drills.

Mackovic, who was known for creatively scripting his offense at the beginning of games, put the Cornhuskers on their heels immediately with an 11-play, 80-yard drive for a touchdown to open the game. Texas had led 20–17 at the half, but when Nebraska took its first lead of the game at 24–23 in the third quarter and then made it 27–23 with 10 minutes remaining in the fourth quarter, things looked bleak for Texas.

The representatives from the Holiday Bowl in San Diego, who had come poised to invite Texas after the 'Horns were dispatched by Nebraska, marveled at the Longhorn Band at halftime and delivered to the Texas representatives material advertising the attractiveness of San Diego as a bowl destination site.

But four plays later, Brown hit receiver Wane McGarity for a 66-yard touchdown pass, and Texas was back in front, 30–27.

Nebraska's ensuing drive stalled at the Longhorn 43, and with 4:41 remaining in the game, Texas got the ball at its own 6. A penalty on the first play pushed the ball back to the 3. Five plays later, Texas had moved the ball to its own 28-yard line. It was fourth down, with inches to go.

Mackovic called timeout and summoned Brown to the sidelines. "Steelers roll left," he said. "Look to run."

Mackovic had used his weapons well in the game. He had taken Ricky Williams, who would win the Heisman Trophy two years later, and used him primarily as a decoy. Priest Holmes, who had been the third back after coming off a knee surgery earlier in his career, had been the workhorse.

Both players, of course, would go on to fame in the NFL, with Holmes becoming the league's top rusher at Kansas City. Holmes finished the game with 120 yards on 11 carries, and Williams carried only 8 times for seven yards. Everybody had seen the pictures of Holmes as he perfected a leap over the middle of the line for short yardage. He had scored four touchdowns that way against North Carolina in the Sun Bowl alone. Nebraska geared to stop Holmes.

And now there was James Brown, right where you left him at the start of this story.

"Look to run," Mackovic had said. But as the team broke the huddle, Brown looked at his tight end, Derek Lewis, and said, "Be ready."

"For what?" Lewis responded, turning to look at his quarterback as he walked out to his position.

"I just might throw it," Brown replied. Brown took the snap, headed to his left, and saw a Nebraska linebacker coming to fill the gap. He also saw something else. There, all alone, seven yards behind the closest defender, stood Derek Lewis.

Seventy thousand fans and a national television audience collectively gasped as Brown suddenly stopped, squared, and flipped the ball to Lewis, who caught it at the Texas 35, turned, and headed toward the goal. Sixty-one yards later, [Lewis] was caught from behind at the Cornhusker 11. Holmes scored his third touchdown of the game to ice it at 37–27 with 1:53 left.

The next morning, Mackovic was on a plane to New York to attend the National Football Foundation College Hall of Fame dinner and to accept on national TV the Fiesta Bowl bid to play Penn State. The reaction and reception he received were amazing. In choosing not to punt from his own 28, thus leaving the game in the hands of his defense with three minutes left, Mackovic had swashbuckled his way into a significant amount of fame. Had it failed, he would have been second-guessed forever because the Cornhuskers would have had the ball only 28 yards from the goal, where a very makeable field-goal attempt would have tied the game, and a touchdown would have won it.

There is an old Texas proverb that says it is only a short distance from the parlor to the outhouse. There was John Mackovic, sitting on a stuffed sofa in the living room on CBS-TV, accepting a bid as the Big 12 representative to the Fiesta Bowl, as Nebraska dropped from national title contention and went to the Orange Bowl.

"The call" seemingly had been seen by everybody in America. Ushers at the David Letterman show were high-fiving the Texas coach, and managers of leading restaurants were sending him complimentary bottles of wine.

James Brown had made good on his promise, even if he didn't quite get the full 21-point margin. He passed for 353 yards, hitting 19 of 28 passes, including the touchdown pass to McGarity. He had led Texas to a stunning victory. The mystique of the North Division of the Big 12 had been shattered, and the guys from the South had proved they belonged.

In the next eight years, Big 12 schools would play in the national championship game five times as the young league quickly solidified itself as a true power in college football.

The victory marked the high-water mark for Mackovic, who was able to enjoy the popularity of "the call" for a short spring and summer. When Brown sprained his ankle in the season opener of 1997 and couldn't play the next week against UCLA, disaster struck. Texas came apart as the Bruins beat the 'Horns, 66–3. Brown never really got well, and neither did his coach. When the Texas season ended at 4–7, Mackovic was removed from the head coaching position and reassigned within the athletics department.

James Brown made a run at arena football and spent some time playing in Europe. In his time at Texas, he had earned a special place. First, he destroyed the myth that an African American couldn't play quarterback at Texas, and second, he had taken "fourth-and-inches" and made it into a euphoria that will forever rank as one of the greatest moments in the storied history of Longhorn football.

Tom Dienhart, *The Sporting News*

LEAPIN' LONGHORNS

*They said it couldn't be done, but Vince Young and the Longhorns ulti-
mately found a way to break USC's 34-game winning streak and wrest
the national title away from the two-time defending champs in the
2006 Rose Bowl.*

Matt Leinart doesn't look good. Please forgive college football's
golden boy. He's fresh from 60 minutes of Texas torture. And he's
toast.

Leinart is barefoot and walking in silence down a lonely hallway.
He isn't dazed and confused. He knows where he is: the Rose Bowl.
And he knows what has happened: Texas beat his Southern
California Trojans to become the national champion. That's why
Leinart marches reluctantly toward the Texas locker room. He
follows the cacophony of celebration and finally finds it.

"Coach Brown! Coach Brown!" Leinart shouts. Texas's Mack
Brown turns and eyes Leinart. A smile creases his face.

"We couldn't stop you guys," Brown whispers into Leinart's ear
as the two embrace after the 41–38 shootout. "That was a classic
game."

Leinart isn't going to argue. He doesn't have the strength. He is
beaten. So is Reggie Bush, who appears from the darkness in
Leinart's wake. He offers a defeated hand to Brown.

"If you're ever in Austin, you look us up," says Brown.

Oh, Brown will be easy to find. He'll be the guy clutching the
crystal football. On this night in Pasadena, he holds it high.

Brown wants to make sure everyone sees it because this
outcome didn't match the predictions. For days that seemed like
months that seemed like years, the Longhorns heard anyone with a
microphone and a can of hairspray yammer about how USC was
one of the greatest teams in college football history. The Rose Bowl
would be the Trojans' coronation. Texas? When the clock struck
midnight, the burnt-orange challengers would turn back into
pumpkins.

"We didn't get much respect from the media on both sides of the ball," Young says.

Instead, the night turned into a big ol' Texas hoedown. And the hoedown hit a high note in the Longhorns' locker room: "Ain't no party like a Longhorn party 'cause a Longhorn party don't stop!" players sang.

No one was going to stop Young from drinking in this moment. It was a national championship game for the ages, supersized with excitement and overloaded with theatrics that had Texas fans two-stepping. Grab somebody—anybody—and dance.

Young danced. He was good, too. He swayed and swiveled. He even gyrated like a halftime performer. And he did it all with that crystal football in his hands.

That's when Young flashed the Heisman pose. He wasn't able to do it for real a month ago, but this was his chance to show USC's two Heisman winners—Leinart and Bush—that he had something even better: the 2005 national championship. Young was the biggest star on the biggest stage in a town that seeps celebrity.

And like every celeb, Young had his star scene. Of course, it came at the climax of this Rose Bowl showdown that had been anticipated since September.

After the Longhorns made a fourth-and-two stop near midfield, everything was in place for Young to morph from hero to legend.

"We knew as soon as we got the ball back, the game was over," safety Michael Huff said.

Facing fourth-and-five from the 8 and only a few ticks clinging to the clock, Young took the snap, looked, looked, looked...no one was open. That's when Vince Young did what Vince Young does best: he ran, angling with purpose toward the right pylon while palming the ball in his right hand. He sprinted across the goal line and into a mass of hysteria and history.

"I said all week that it would come down to the last play of the game, and it did," Young said.

Funny thing is, everyone stuffed in the stands knew what was coming on that play. The security guy in the yellow jacket, the Rose Bowl official in the striking white suit, the USC song girl—they all knew Vince Young was going to run. Didn't matter what happened.

"It's disturbing, particularly when you know what the problem is and you can't solve it," USC coach Pete Carroll said. "It's his factor of running that made the difference."

And just like that, USC's run was done. The 34-game winning streak? Over. The three-peat? A two-peat. Bush? Gone to the NFL (likely along with running back LenDale White and possibly other Trojans who still have eligibility).

Texas had no time to weep for USC. This was too new for the 'Horns even to consider next season. The Longhorns hadn't won a national championship since 1970.

That's years of woulda-shoulda-couldas served with two scoops of "wait till next year"—enough to turn the stomach of any Texas-loving fan who could recite the pain and suffering the past 35 years had wrought:

- The 1984 Cotton Bowl meltdown against Georgia.
- The 2001 Big 12 title game flop against Colorado.
- The Oklahoma losses under Mack Brown. Pick one.
- The John Mackovic era. And David McWilliams. Ugh.

But this night wasn't about the past. And it wasn't about next year, when Young will be in the NFL. This night was all about the here and now and a national title for Texas. In 1970, the Longhorns shared the title and finished with a blemish when they lost in the Cotton Bowl to Notre Dame. Page back to 1969 to find the last time the Longhorns finished unbeaten and on top of the college football world. In an interesting twist, that Texas team was the last all-white squad to win a national championship. Thirty-six years later, a black quarterback was the centerpiece of the program's return to the pinnacle.

Everyone wanted a piece of that action on this chilly California night. Actor and Texas alum Matthew McConaughey behaved like a freshman at a fraternity party. He leaped, yelled, hugged, and hollered. No one heard him, but everyone saw him. A giant Texas player waved a giant Texas flag. People cried on the 35-yard line. Cheerleaders ran in delight—and in fear of being trampled by the horde that hounded Young. Surely, this must have been what it was like for Elvis.

Young wasn't ready to leave the building, but he needed sanctuary in the locker room to digest it all. Had Texas just pulled off a title game upset that ranks with Miami's toppling Nebraska in the 1984 Orange Bowl, Penn State's tripping Miami in the 1987 Fiesta Bowl, and Ohio State's takedown of Miami in the 2003 Fiesta Bowl? No doubt. And even better: Young outplayed Leinart, his more bally-hooed and beloved counterpart.

But there's no rivalry between the two. Before Leinart limped away from the Texas locker room for another lonely stroll, Young grabbed him. They said the usual nicey-nice stuff winners and losers chat about while wearing dirty uniforms in half-lit hallways. But before Leinart left, Young grabbed paper and a pencil. He wanted to get Leinart's cell phone number.

Hey, you never know when these two will meet again. But until then, maybe they'll want to talk more about what went on during a magical night in Pasadena.

Quarterback Vince Young brought the Longhorns their first national title in decades with this flashy Rose Bowl performance over USC in the January 8, 2006, Rose Bowl in Pasadena.

Section II
THE PLAYERS

Cora Oltersdorf, *The Alcalde*

AMERICA'S COACH

Before he was "America's Coach," Tom Landry was a star Longhorn. Originally a quarterback, he deferred to Bobby Layne's hold on that position and made his mark as a safety, although he was utilized at other positions on both offense and defense.

The joke goes that there are only three sports in Texas: high school football, college football, and professional football. But the Dallas Cowboys became the national kings of football not only by winning, but also because of their beloved first coach, Tom Landry. He elevated his profession through his high standards of conduct and integrity. "He was a great American, a great leader, always loyal to the University of Texas, and a friend to those he knew," says Frank Denius, an Austin lawyer, businessman, and civic leader who met Landry as a student.

Though Landry had been out of the limelight for more than 10 years when he died of leukemia on February 12, 2000, public reaction was strong and emotional. He was an ideal, the quiet, dignified coach who people trusted, someone who could go up against the biggest ego not because he had one even bigger, but because he had integrity that no ego could match.

Landry is synonymous with the Dallas Cowboys, whom he coached for 28 seasons. Associated Press sportswriter Jamie Aron put [Landry's] tenure in perspective when he wrote that coach Tom Coughlin of the Jacksonville Jaguars "would have to remain in place through 2023 to match Landry."

But the Cowboys were third on [Landry's] ordered priority list of God, family, and football. Everyone knows of his list. He wrote it on the blackboard at the beginning of training camp, and his friends, fans, and the press can quote it.

Landry became a born-again Christian in 1959 and devoted much of his time outside of football to Christian organizations, such as the Fellowship of Christian Athletes, and to helping Billy Graham and other religious leaders. Even as a famous coach, he still went door to door to ask for pledges for his church. He was married to his college sweetheart, Alicia, for 50 years, and had three children—Tom Jr., Lisa, and Kitty.

Despite his famous stone-faced exterior, he was open and caring. Ralph "Peppy" Blount, a friend and former Longhorn teammate, says, "He was an inspiration and not a recluse at all. He shared his life and made himself available to anyone."

Dave Braden attended the same church as Landry, Highland Park Methodist, where one of Landry's public memorial services took place ([Landry had been] a member for 43 years). Braden says, "On one occasion, Tom gave a layman's sermon that was very impressive—not because Tom was such a good speaker, but because he was so sincere." The sermon came after his daughter, Lisa Childress, died of liver cancer in 1995. (Braden did not know Landry at UT, but they met when Landry sold insurance to make ends meet in his early days as the Cowboys coach, before coaching was a full-time job. Landry made sales calls on Braden because he knew Braden's brother-in-law from the Aviation Student Program during World War II.)

Small-Town Boy Makes Good

As a boy, Ray Landry had moved on his doctor's recommendation from Illinois to balmy Mission, Texas, 10 miles from Mexico. Ray's health improved enough for him to play high school football. He moved away for college, then returned to the Rio Grande Valley to make his living as a mechanic and esteemed member of the local volunteer fire department. He married his high school sweetheart, Ruth. In 1924, Tommy Landry, as his friends called him, was born, the third of four children.

Mission takes great pride in Tom Landry: the town named the high school stadium after him. (His father got a park.) It commissioned a downtown mural honoring him, near a street named after him. (Several Cowboys embedded their footprints in the cement in front of the mural.)

After he played on the 1941 championship high school football team, Landry headed to UT the following year. However, national duty called, and he entered the Army Air Corps after one semester of college. He flew 30 missions over Europe as a B-17 bomber pilot, surviving one crash landing in Czechoslovakia. (His older brother Robert died in a B-17.)

Landry returned to the university in 1945 and settled into campus life, more mature than the first time around. He joined Delta Kappa Epsilon fraternity and the football team. He was heavily involved in intramural sports, excelling in wrestling, basketball, and swimming.

Longhorn teammate and star receiver Peppy Blount remembers Landry well. They both married Tri-Delt sorority sisters and played football together for three years. "He was a very fine fellow, never loud," Blount says. "Tommy was just like the Rock of Gibraltar."

Blount recalls their initiation into the Cowboys, a service group comprised mainly of fraternity members. They were hauled out to somewhere near Barton Springs, stripped bare, blindfolded, and covered in molasses and Post Toasties. The members then made the initiates get on their hands and knees and crawl around in a circle, singing the whole time. It finally dawned on the group that the members had left them out there without clothes or a ride home. They ran to the freeway where a kind soul let them into the bed of his pickup truck and drove them home. "The entire time," Blount remembers, "Tommy maintained his dignity.

"That is," he adds, "at least as much as anyone can under those kinds of circumstances."

Along with his bedrock integrity and moral strength, it didn't hurt that Landry was a great football player. The April 1946 *Alcalde* took notice of him while sizing up the upcoming football season's prospects after spring practice: "Tommy Landry...revealed himself as one of the best all-around backfield prospects in several seasons. He can pass, kick, and run—especially pass."

He played quarterback in high school, but the Longhorns' star quarterback, Bobby Layne, precluded Landry from playing that position. For the sake of getting into the game, [Landry] made a position switch and ended up a safety. He played various positions during his years on the Longhorn team: fullback, defensive halfback (now called a cornerback), and kicker.

In 1948, Landry's senior year, he was elected cocaptain (with Dick Harris) because of both his playing skill and coolness under pressure. It was a disappointing season, and though the team received a surprise invitation to attend the Orange Bowl, they initially turned it down. According to Blount, it took some "bribing" from athletics director D. X. Bible to get them to accept the invitation: a vacation to Havana, Cuba, for the team, coaching staff, and their families. Before the game, the Longhorns had been dubbed "a third-rate team," but they trounced Bobby Dodd's Georgia Tech Bulldogs, 41–28, in a remarkable victory.

After graduating with a BBA in 1949, Landry joined the New York Giants and became the equivalent of their defensive coordinator while still a player. In December 1959, Clint Murchison and Bedford Wynne, while waiting to receive an NFL expansion franchise, signed Landry to be head coach of a nonexistent team. The Cowboys played their first game on August 19, 1960, the start of a horrid season with 11 losses; a tie was their best showing. The Cowboys played badly over the next four years, and public criticism was particularly harsh when Landry's contract came up. However, Murchison signed him for another 10 years despite very little to support his faith in Landry. That would come later.

Landry was known for his stone face and a complete lack of outward emotion, no matter which direction the game was going. He kept his distance from his players so he could maintain objectivity in case he had to fire someone. When asked if he'd ever seen Landry smile, former Cowboys running back Walt Garrison replied no, "but I was only there nine years."

Despite his stoic demeanor, Landry cared a great deal about his team and was fiercely competitive. His players recall seeing him smile after the first Super Bowl win, a great relief after many agonizing years of coaching a team that was not quite good enough to win anything more than a regular-season game. He remained the same person, even after such ego-expanding events as when the Cowboys were named "America's Team" and had 20 straight winning seasons.

David Romness, a journalism senior who played golf with Landry during the Ex-Students' Association's 50-Year Reunion, says, "He was really quiet and nice. If you didn't know who he was, you wouldn't have known he was anybody."

Braden saw Landry laugh more than once at the reunion of which he was honorary chairman, and says, "For those who think Tom was so serious and he never laughed or smiled, I can only vouch for the fact that off the field he had a great sense of humor."

Landry checked into a hospital a few short weeks after the reunion and was diagnosed with chronic myelogenous leukemia, which only occurs in about 5,000 people per year. The disease causes an overproduction of white blood cells, which don't allow the body to produce enough red blood cells, which are vital to carrying oxygen to every part of the body.

According to Braden, Landry displayed a calm demeanor during the reunion, one of his last public appearances. "Obviously he was already very ill," says Braden, "but he was there for UT and his class, and not a word was spoken about it."

Landry the Innovator

So much is made of Tom Landry's distinctive character that the innovations that made him famous are sometimes overlooked. Landry specialized in defense, and Blount says that Landry was an innovator when it came to revising existing defenses. He used the "4-4-2-1 defense," so called because it dropped two ends off the standard defensive lineup, resulting in four linemen, four linebackers, two cornerbacks, and one safety. "Nobody knew blocking assignments against something like that," says Blount.

Landry created the "flex defense," which placed a tackle a half-yard behind the other tackle, and in 1956, the "4-3 defense," which was so good that five years later he had to create the "multiple set offense," involving his trademark offensive line shift, to counter it. The lineman would head to the line of scrimmage and set down, then stand to hide the players behind them, who were quickly changing positions, before resetting (called a "chorus line"). This went against all standards of play. Ordinarily, teams ran the same offense on every play. But with the multiple set offense, the opposing team didn't know what was going on in the middle of the play and who was in which position.

His techniques became industry standards because they worked. Over the course of 28 seasons, Landry won 270 games, the third-most in NFL history (behind Don Shula and George Halas). The Cowboys made 18 playoff appearances, won 13 division championships, and went to five Super Bowls, winning numbers VI (1972) and XII (1978).

Landry won the Ex-Students' Association's Distinguished Alumnus Award in 1973, the Horatio Alger Award in 1983, and was inducted into the Pro Football Hall of Fame in 1990 and the Dallas Cowboys Ring of Honor in 1993. For the Ring of Honor, a miniature fedora hangs beside Landry's name instead of a player's jersey number.

As for his trademark headgear, it started out simply as a way to keep warm. Landry continued wearing it because it conveyed a professional image.

Everyone loved Landry, but it would take an unexpected firing to let Landry know how much. When Jerry Jones bought the Cowboys in 1988, his first act was to call Landry, who was on an Austin golf course, and unceremoniously fire him. Dallas held a "Hats Off to Tom Landry!" Day, with 100,000 fans gathering at Texas Stadium at noon for a celebration that lasted through the night with a ball and concert. In response, Landry cried over what he termed one of the "most exciting and meaningful" days in his life.

After he lost his nine-month fight against cancer, Dallas once again stepped up to remind everyone that Tom Landry was not a forgotten hero. Seemingly within hours there was an Internet petition drive to rename Texas Stadium for him, an effort that is ongoing at press time. [Editor's Note: in 2006, the name had not changed.]

On a rainy February 17, 2000, 800 people attended a semiprivate memorial at Landry's church, Highland Park Baptist [Methodist]. And fans waited for hours to attend a second, public memorial at the Meyerson Symphony Center, where 1,500 people came to pay their last respects. Braden, who lives in Dallas, says, "I have never seen such an outpouring of true affection for another human being as our community has lavished on his memory."

In Mission, locals left impromptu memorials at Landry's mural, and the town held its own memorial service.

After the private family funeral, Landry's son placed a gray fedora into the casket before it was closed to be buried at Sparkman-Hillcrest Memorial Park, sending Landry to gather what former wide receiver Drew Pearson called God's Football League.

Bob St. John, *The Sporting News*

ROPING STEERS WON'T BE EASY WITH NOBIS ROAMING THE RANGE

Although he finished seventh in balloting for the Heisman Trophy, line-backer Tommy Nobis became the first Texas player to win the Maxwell Award, another award honoring the nation's top football player, in 1965, the year this article appeared in The Sporting News.

This city literally vibrates with football, and if you are here and it does not affect you, then you are not affected by anything.

And nobody feels this vibration more than Tommy Nobis, the Texas Longhorns' All-American linebacker-guard. He talks of it and of dedication and devotion and school spirit with such sincerity, and of his accomplishments with such modesty, that he seems unreal.

I watched him and listened to him and, at any moment, I expected him to disappear into the air with Mary Poppins or [I'd] turn away for a minute and find that Tommy had gone and then hear, "Hi-yo, Silver, a-a-a-a-a-way!" But he is real.

For this young man is totally dedicated to being the best guard-linebacker in the country and to making the University of Texas the best football team. And he is probably the best linebacker ever to play in the Southwest Conference.

His feats are already legendary. They are discussed authoritatively here from under the coolness of the trees in Scholtz Bier Garten to the hallowed halls of the capitol building.

High Praise from Dietzel

Darrell Royal says he has never had a better or more dedicated football player than Nobis. Army's Paul Dietzel, who learned [about Nobis] last fall, calls him the best linebacker he has even seen in college football. And SMU's Hayden Fry says, "Tommy Nobis is a once-in-a-lifetime kid. He's a perfect type youngster. One boy like Tommy can make the difference in winning and losing."

Nobis looks the part. He now weighs 235 pounds, or 20 pounds more than last season (however, there is a movement afoot in the conference to make him illegal unless he loses weight), and it is 235 pounds of muscle. They say his hair is red, but it is really orange, appropriately, and his skin also has a dash of orange coloring and freckles dot his face. His neck measures 19".

His face and general appearance transmit a certain straightness, as if he had just run into a brick wall. I don't doubt that the brick wall is now in shambles.

When he first began playing football for Texas a few years and 35 pounds ago, Tommy was pretty shy. But this has changed, too...for the most part. The limelight has a way of doing this to—or for—you.

Tommy Feels Fortunate

"Well, my life has certainly changed," said Tommy. "But I just feel fortunate people are so interested in me. I just wish I was about half as good as some people have written and said that I am.

"People spot me pretty easily because of my red hair (orange), and they come up to me just about anywhere I go and want to talk football. That's fine with me. I mean, engineers talk about engineering.

"Football is my life. I'll talk anybody's ear off about it.

"Aw, they ask me to make speeches sometimes now, too. That was tough at first, but I...just start talking football and it's fine."

Rumor has it around here that Tommy has become very proficient at speech-making. Once, after last fall, he moved a teammate so much that he said, "Tommy, I never realized you could make a talk like that."

"Oh," answered Tommy, "what do you think I am...just another pretty face?"

"He still keeps things to himself a lot," explained Marvin Kristynik, his roommate and cocaptain. "I ask him over and over if he has a steady girl, and he just shuffles around and won't say. I finally had to ask her, and you know, he does."

"Aw," interrupted Nobis, avoiding specifics.

Football is much more specific for him. And, perhaps, you must go back to the time Nobis first came to Jefferson High School in San Antonio to find out what makes him run.

"Gee, that kid came here at 140 pounds and ran the 50-yard dash in seven flat," said his coach at Jefferson, Pat Shannon.

"It was something inside him. The kid had character. He was proud, loyal, and dedicated and had an instinct for the football. You don't coach a thing like that."

Caught Bus at 5:00 AM

Nobis lived out in the Jefferson district, so he caught the bus at 5:00 AM every day to attend the school, and after practice, he'd catch the bus again and wouldn't get back home until 8:30 PM—some dedication.

"Kids can get by on great ability or on real toughness," continued Shannon, "but add loyalty and dedication to that, and they become great. Tommy is great. I think you'd have to start with Tommy's parents. You'll never meet finer people. That's where he got his fine character...at home."

Nobis still pinches himself when he thinks what has happened.

"I just know I'm extremely fortunate to be here," he explained. "I'd always followed Texas when I was in high school and had dreams, like all kids have, of being an All-American and playing with a great team. But I still can't believe it all.

"I thought when I was a senior in high school that I'd be lucky to get a scholarship to a small school. My grades weren't so good. I had an English teacher at Jeff who advised me not to come here. She said she didn't think I could do passing work.

"I worried and worried what to do, and then just told myself, 'Well, if you don't give it a try, you'll always wonder.' Well, the books have been a struggle ever since, but I've gotten by. Heck, I've never fooled myself. I know I'm not so smart in books. I know my career is football."

He's Easy to Spot

Nobis has always been easy to find on the field because you ordinarily watch the ball carrier and Tommy is the one draped around him.

Many times when he meets a runner with his straight-up tackle, the offense wonders what to call next, a play or a doctor.

"Play recognition is the big thing for a linebacker," said Tommy. "Our coaches are a tremendous help finding keys for us. I'm not fast. … I look for the keys. No, I can't say I play mad. I just can't help getting fired up. I dunno. … I hear the crowd and all, and my blood starts roaring. Well, sometimes I get mad if I mess up or get clipped.

"Of course, it's an individual thing, too. You hate for a guy to get the best of you.

"My girl (there, it's out) and my mother always tell me before a game, 'Now. Tommy, be careful, but play a good game.' Good gosh! Now how can you be careful and play a good game? A guy can't worry about getting hurt. You just do the best you can and then you shouldn't have time to worry about it."

Like he said, he can talk your ear off about football at Texas. And it is sincere talk by a very sincere guy.

Neil Amdur, *The New York Times*

RESERVE QUARTERBACK PUTS TEXAS ON DREAM STREET

James Street took over at quarterback at Texas during the 1968 season and began a run of success that brought the Steers their first national championship the following season. The New York Times featured him in this story a day before he led them to victory in the 1970 Cotton Bowl against Notre Dame.

On fourth down at the Texas 43-yard line late in the fourth quarter, with Arkansas leading 14–8, James Street called timeout and walked to the sideline for a strategy session with Coach Darrell Royal.

"Run the 52 veer pass," the Texas coach told his dark-haired quarterback after consulting by phone with assistant coaches in the press box.

Street, a serious, high-strung senior, turned toward the field, then ran back to Royal for a second look. "The 52 veer pass," he knew, meant a long pattern with only one receiver, Randy Peschel, the tight end, going downfield. And the play hadn't worked all year.

"Are you sure?" Street said, with a sheepish glance for questioning Royal's judgment.

Royal nodded again, and Street ran back to the huddle for the play that would make or break the Texas season.

"Fifty-two veer pass," Street told his teammates in firm tones.

The helmet of Bob McKay, a 6'6" offensive tackle and all-America choice, snapped up.

"Damn it, Street, you can't throw the ball that far," McKay said, breaking a standing Texas rule about no conversations in the huddle.

Street repeated the call.

"Okay," McKay said, "but everybody better cover like on a punt."

Texas completed the fourth-down pass play for a 44-yard gain, scored the go-ahead touchdown, and went on to a dramatic 15–14 victory over Arkansas in a game viewed on national television. As with most legends in the Lone Star State, the stories behind the gamble and who said what have grown taller with each passing day.

What is not a tall tale, however, is James Street, the Longhorns' 5'11" tricaptain who, like another East Texas–bred quarterback under Royal, James Saxton, prefers the first name James to Jim or Jimmy.

Since replacing Bill Bradley at quarterback in the third game of the 1968 season, Street and Texas have won all 19 games. A victory over Notre Dame in the Cotton Bowl Thursday would assure the Longhorns of all claims to the national championship.

"We weren't winning then," Royal said today of his decision to make Street the number-one quarterback. "So we tried to change something. Why does a manager relieve a pitcher?"

There is more pitcher in Street, a product of Longview, Texas, than most rivals realize. In two years with the Texas baseball team while missing spring football drills, Street has won 21 games, lost only six, posted an impressive earned-run average of 1.34, hurled the first no-hitter in the Southwest Conference in 14 years, helped the Longhorns to a pair of league championships, and won second-team all-America recognition.

Street has such an intense competitive desire that he quit playing charity basketball games with a group of Austin disk jockeys because he did not like the idea of having to lose every game.

Ted Koy, a running back, recalled another incident in a huddle during Street's first game at quarterback. "He was yelling about guts and pride and telling us to pull ourselves together," said Koy, a journalism major, who writes an interesting column for the school newspaper. "Then he said, 'Okay, on two—ready, break.' Well, in the course of all that talk, he forgot to call the play."

Such mental errors have not happened since. In fact, Street has become one of the squad's glib spirits.

After bringing Texas from a 14–0 deficit to a 27–17 victory over Oklahoma earlier this year, Street was asked whether Royal had called all the plays. "Yep," said Street, whose striking features bear a resemblance to Elvis Presley. "But I had the same plays in mind."

* * *

Editor's note: the big play was correctly known as the 53 veer pass.

Blackie Sherrod, *Dallas Morning News*

REQUIEM FOR AN ALL-AMERICAN

Less than a week after helping Texas beat Arkansas in the 1969 battle to be number one, safety Freddie Joe Steinmark was hospitalized with a tumor on his left leg, which had to be amputated. He attended the Cotton Bowl victory over Notre Dame on crutches and became an inspiration to cancer victims, continuing his classes and becoming a popular spokesman and fund-raiser for cancer research. He also found time to help coach freshman defensive backs. However, his illness spread, and he died on June 6, 1971. The following day, the legendary Blackie Sherrod penned this touching tribute. The following introduction ran with the article: "Legendary Blackie Sherrod, whose Sunday 'Scattershooting' column has been a Sports Day staple for the past 18 years, retired recently. On upcoming Sundays, the Morning News will run some of Blackie's best columns from his more than 50 years of sports writing. The following is Sherrod's column from June 7, 1971."

Six months after they took the left leg of Freddie Steinmark, he returned to the Houston tumor clinic for another of his nerve-wracking check-ups. The little Texas safety had to do this every three months, as do all victims of osteogenic sarcoma. He underwent blood tests and X-rays to determine if the dread malignancy might appear in other parts of his strong young body.

For several nights preceding his trips to M.D. Anderson Cancer Center, Freddie would stare at the ceiling. He knew the odds. He prayed for a miracle.

"They told me not to worry, but that's easy for them to say," Freddie said. "They're the ones taking the X-rays, not the ones getting them."

When Freddie would get a clean report, he would return joyously to the Texas campus and throw himself into another project with fierce energy. He took up golf, balancing himself on one leg while he swung. He learned to water ski. He went religiously to the Longhorn weight room to build up the rest of his body, as if muscle could hold off any return invasion of cancer cells. He worked his grades back to a B average. He made speeches and appearances. He wanted feverish activity to keep his mind occupied so it wouldn't wander back to the calendar and the date of his next trip to Houston.

Last July a couple blurs showed up on X-rays of Freddie's lungs. It could be one of several things, the doctors told Freddie; we'll watch it close. A bit later, they told Freddie he would have to start a series of chemotherapy treatments. He didn't change expression. But he guarded the news as if it were the atomic secret. He wanted no one to know. It was almost as if Freddie thought the treatments were a sign of personal weakness. The news might bring pity from his teammates and friends, and above all, he didn't want that.

The chemotherapy consisted of six days of shots that, hopefully, would kill or arrest any fast-growing cancer cells. They make the patient frightfully nauseous. But he masked the trips and treatments from all save a precious few. Scott Henderson, the linebacker and Freddie's apartment mate, knew, but he respected the confidence.

One possible side-effect of chemotherapy shots is the loss of hair. Freddie had a long, thick black mane, and he was proud of it. His teammates teasingly accused him of being a hippie. Okay, you guys, he said. I'm gonna help coach the freshman defensive backs, and just to show you how seriously I'm taking this job, I'll get rid of the hippy image. I'll get rid of all this hair. As a matter of fact, I'll just shave it all off, just to show you I'm not kidding.

So the Texas squad had a little ceremony in the locker room, and they all laughed and cheered as Bobby Wuensch shaved off the Steinmark hair. His teammates didn't realize he dreamed up this little act to hide the fact he was taking treatment that made his hair fall out. He kept his head shaved. Rick Troberman took note of the bald head and the missing leg and applied the nickname "Pirate." Freddie went along with the gag. He had his ear pierced and wore a gold ring in it for a while.

He shared his worry and concern with no one. But sometimes when you were in a conversation with Freddie, he would be staring at you vacantly with those enormous black eyes and there would be silence, and he would say, "Excuse me, I guess I wasn't listening. What did you say?"

To the last, Freddie refused to accept the idea that the cancer had caught up with him and finally dragged him down. When he was hospitalized this last time in M.D. Anderson, he believed—at least outwardly—that he was there to have some fluid removed from his body. When his priest from Austin, Father Fred Bomar, walked quietly into Room 514W and sat down, Freddie looked at him narrowly.

"Have you got some business in Houston, Father?" he said. The priest said no, he just came down for a visit.

"Do you know something I don't know?" asked Freddie. The priest said no.

His friends thought it was rather a miracle, Freddie having played regularly on a national championship team with the tumor already gnawing at his leg. He had survived the amputation and returned to active life, had been able to move back into society, to tell people how he felt, to squeeze another 17 months out of precious life. Freddie didn't think it was a miracle: it was what an athlete was supposed to do. Now that same fierce competition kept him hanging on for days, weeks, after the average person would have let go. Doctors walked out of his room with tears in their eyes.

Two weeks ago, I visited the room. The shades were drawn. A television set suspended from the ceiling, with the volume off, flickered lifelessly with a soap opera. There was a skinny couch with bed pillows along one wall, where Freddie's mother, Gloria, and his girl friend, Linda Wheeler, spent each day, and his father spent each night. A vigil candle on a table burned 24 hours a day. Freddie was a gaunt shadow and his voice was about gone, and I had to bend close to hear him whisper, "I'm getting better."

Freddie has written a book about his experiences. It will be published this fall. The editor noticed after Freddie was hospitalized that he had not made a dedication of the book, and he asked to whom Freddie wanted to dedicate his story. Freddie said to the Lord, who had been so good to him.

Emily Nasits, http://www.earlcampbell.com

EARL CAMPBELL: THE COLLEGE YEARS

In 1977 Earl Campbell became the first Longhorn to capture the Heisman Trophy. In his senior season, "the Tyler Rose" piled up more than 1700 yards rushing, pushing his career total to more than 4400 yards with 41 touchdowns.

Like most wide-eyed freshmen, Earl Campbell arrived at the University of Texas with mixed emotions. He was excited about his decision to become a Longhorn, his academic and athletic future at UT, and the growing opportunity to meet new people. After all, Earl had rarely traveled beyond the outskirts of Tyler, the small East Texas town he had grown up in his entire life. Thus, Earl was also apprehensive as he walked across the beautiful yet extremely large and overwhelming campus. Earl arrived on the 357-acre campus with only one pair of jeans, a couple of T-shirts, one suit that his high school sweetheart and future wife, Reuna, had sewn for him, and only $40 in his pocket.

Little did he or the rest of the world know, Earl Campbell, the young, fresh-faced kid from humble beginnings, was about to change the face of Texas football and become one of the most influential athletes this world has ever known. His decision to sign with the University of Texas would change Earl's life forever.

The freshman recruiting class of 1974 was considered to be one of the best crops of athletes Darrell K. Royal ever recruited...and it would, unfortunately, be one of his last.

Included in this class were Campbell, Rick Ingraham, Alfred Jackson, and the future Outland Trophy winner, Brad Shearer. The "rookie"class was led by an outstanding team of veterans, including Earl's player host on his official visit, Raymond Clayborn, and [Earl's] new friend, Roosevelt Leaks. These young men were looked upon as the future of Texas football and [it was hoped that they would] restore the dynasty back to greatness. After all, in the 11 years prior to Earl's arrival, Texas had won three national championships, in 1963, 1969, and 1970. The expectations were high for the entire team—on the football field and in the classroom.

Upon the realization that he was being looked at as just another "dumb jock," Earl decided that he was going to prove everyone wrong. Not only did he attend every class on his schedule, but he also sat in the front row, directly in front of the teacher. He felt it was a privilege to be granted the opportunity to walk away from Texas with a degree in hand.

The 1974 football season provided a year of "firsts" for Earl: his first home game, touchdown, loss, OU rivalry, 100-yard game, and battle against Texas A&M. His first collegiate game was at Boston College on September 14, 1974. Although Earl was understandably nervous, he didn't show it on the field, rushing for 85 yards on 13 carries and leading his 'Horns to a 42–19 victory over their host from Massachusetts.

The Boston College game was an important ice-breaker for Earl, but nothing could have prepared him for the experience of his first home game at Memorial Stadium in front of more than 75,000 screaming fans sporting burnt orange and white. His team mentors, Clayborn and Leaks, tried to prepare him for the dazed excitement they knew he would feel, but as Earl rushed from the field house to take the field, he couldn't believe his eyes. He never imagined the Texas fans would ever fill the large stadium and couldn't believe how loud they were screaming. His nervous energy quickly turned to on-field domination, however, as the young freshman rushed for 85 yards and his first collegiate touchdown, leading his team to a 34–7 victory over Wyoming. His first home game in a Longhorn uniform was a complete athletic success.

With his impressive freshman year performance, racking up 928 yards rushing in the regular season, Earl received the Southwest Conference Newcomer of the Year Award. More importantly, however, Earl successfully passed all of his classes that year and declared speech communications as his major.

The next year would bring many positive experiences to Earl Campbell's life. Not only did Earl find himself at the pinnacle of a successful collegiate career, but he was also much more comfortable with his life in Austin. During his freshman year, he had found himself extremely homesick, missing his family and friends back home in Tyler.

But with the addition of his twin brothers, Tim and Steve, to the Longhorn football family at the beginning of the 1975 season, Earl was excited about having family close to him in Austin. He also established a familial relationship with his coach and mentor, Darrell Royal. He often visited Royal and his wife, Edith, at home and also became very close with their personal friends, especially Ernest and Joyce Owens, who owned a customized Longhorn Trailways bus that provided a great place for their friends to tailgate in before and after football games. The importance of friends and family, a value instilled in Earl at a young age by his mother and best friend, Ann Campbell, was always so important to Earl. Ann extended that family bond to the Royal family, as well. She would often write Coach Royal letters of encouragement during the season, promising that she would always keep Royal in her prayers.

The 'Horns finished the 1975 season with an impressive 11–2 record, including a win over Colorado in the Bluebonnet Bowl. Earl was voted the Bluebonnet Offensive Player of the Game Award, while his freshman brother, Tim, was named the Defensive Player of the Game. Earl was also named to the All-Southwest Conference and All-American teams, and he achieved his goal of rushing for more than 1,000 yards in a single season.

While the 1975 season brought an extreme amount of personal and athletic success to Earl's life, his junior year was quite a different story. During summer practice, Earl took a pitchout from the quarterback, cut outside, and began running up the field. He was stopped short of his destination—but not by his tough defensive teammates. Earl heard a pop in his leg that sent him crashing to the grass. In his many years of playing football, he had never felt the kind of pain he was experiencing during that moment. The unstoppable "Tyler Rose" had torn a hamstring. Unfortunately, there are no immediate remedies for this injury. Earl had to accept this and begin to prepare for a long season of recovery. Although he was advised by the team doctors to rest and recover his leg for the first game, Earl was determined not to disappoint his team, the fans, or himself. His effort would go unfounded, however. Injured, Earl rushed for only 23 yards on five carries, and the 'Horns suffered a tough defeat, 14–13, at the hands of a lesser Boston College team. And if that opening-game loss wasn't tough enough to swallow, Earl and the Longhorns experienced one of their most embarrassing losses ever when they let North Texas State defeat them, 17–14, the next week. Although still in severe pain from his hamstring tear, Earl reeled out one of his best games against North Texas State, racking up 208 yards on 32 carries and even scoring one touchdown. But it would not be enough on this day.

The remainder of the season continued to be epitomized by solid ups and downs. The 'Horns finished the season 5–51 and in fifth place in the Southwest Conference. This included a hard-fought battle against Oklahoma that ended in a 6–6 tie, a tough loss against archrival Texas A&M at home in Memorial Stadium, and a rewarding victory against Arkansas, 29–12, a game in which Earl gave an unyielding effort, amassing 131 yards and two touchdowns. But that final, satisfying victory proved bittersweet, as the 'Horns finished their worst season since 1956, the year before Darrell Royal become head coach of the Texas Longhorns.

Throughout the season, Coach Royal suffered severe criticism at the hands of a fickle media. Only one year prior, they were singing his praises, but this year was a different story. The members of the media began to doubt Royal's decision-making capabilities and questioned his age and ability to relate to his young players. This constant abuse prompted Earl to respond, "I don't pay attention to what y'all are saying 'cause I was always taught by my parents to respect my elders, and I'm gonna do just that. My job is to do what I'm told and play football. That's the least I can do for Coach Royal since he's the one responsible for me being where I'm at today." But despite the support and respect Coach Royal received from his players and fans, including Earl, Royal knew it was time to step down as head coach at the University of Texas.

After the Arkansas win, Earl stood in the back of the locker room on a folding chair, listening as his mentor, friend, and beloved coach addressed the "changing times" in the sport and admitted that the hardest part about leaving the program would be saying good-bye to all his players and assistant coaches, including "Earl Campbell, who is definitely in a league of his own." To this day, Royal reflects on that day, fondly recalling that Earl was the only player who stayed during his entire retirement announcement.

Earl was devastated by the thought of playing for any other coach than the one he considered to be the best coach in the history of the game, Coach Darrell Royal. That night as Earl was leaving the stadium, he saw two men who he had never met before hugging each other good-bye and saying, "I love you." Earl had never witnessed two males openly expressing their feelings for one another. This prompted Earl to find the Owens's Trailways bus. He knew he would find Coach Royal there with his friends. He entered the bus, walked over to Royal, explained what he had just witnessed, and said, "This touched me 'cause I didn't know what I was gonna say to you tonight in the event I saw you. Anyway, I just want you to know that no matter what happens, I'll always love you."

To this day, Royal describes Earl as "a loyal, caring friend. When Earl Campbell takes someone as a friend, there's nothing he wouldn't do for them."

Earl's senior year, the 1977 football season would test his determination, strength, willpower, and faith in God. After being hired as Royal's successor, Fred Akers decided to meet with every football player on the team, including Earl. One day, after the two men had finished taking pictures for the media guide, Akers asked Earl to step into his office.

He asked Earl if he "wanted to run the ball at this university." Earl, of course, answered that he did. Akers went on to explain that he wanted to change the offense from a wishbone attack to a straight-back formation and desired Earl to be the focal point, carrying the ball 35 to 40 times during each game. Earl was familiar with the offense from his years at John Tyler High School and declared to Akers that he could handle the formation.

Akers said, "Good, Mr. Campbell. You're going to have to prove it to me, and it's going to take an awful lot of hard work on your part. I want you down to 220 pounds by the time the season begins. That's a key ingredient if this is going to work."

Earl was stunned. He'd weighed almost 245 pounds for several years and had no idea if he could shed that much weight in such a short period of time. But determined to make his team successful and respect Coach Akers's wishes, Earl decided to visit Frank Medina, the Longhorns' infamous trainer. Medina had served with two different Olympic teams and was nationally respected as one of the best athletic trainers in the world. Earl began to train with Medina every morning at 6:30 AM, pounding the heavy bag in a rubber sweat suit, running track for an hour, lifting weights, and doing 400 sit-ups while wearing a weighted vest. Then it was off to the sauna for more than a half-hour. He would attend his classes for a few hours and then participate in practice for the remainder of the evening. Although he thought it would be virtually impossible, Earl Campbell reported for the first home game at 220 pounds. With his hard work and determination throughout the preseason, Earl inspired his teammates to "step up" their game as well. He also began to think more and more about winning the infamous Heisman Trophy, awarded to the best collegiate athlete in the country. Earl had never even heard of the Heisman when he visited Texas for the first time while still in high school. But now the Heisman was definitely in his reach...if he continued to work hard, lead his teammates to victory, and bring the national spotlight back to Texas.

After opening the season with a 44–0 thrashing of Boston College at home, the 'Horns went on to defeat their next two opponents, Virginia and Rice, with a combined score of 140–15. Although they were clearly on a roll, the sportswriters continued to doubt the 'Horns because they had not beaten any tough teams. The first real test would be the annual Texas versus Oklahoma rivalry. After two starting Texas quarterbacks went down in the first half, Randy McEachern, who had always worked out mainly with the practice squad, was forced to step in at signal caller. This opened the door for Earl, in a way, as the team was now dependent on their running game. One of the most exciting plays of the game would also be the infamous run that would thrust Earl into the national "Heisman hype." After the handoff, Earl cut right and saw a dead end. He then reversed, hurdled an Oklahoma defensive player, and exploded down the field for a 25-yard touchdown score.

After that run and Earl's first ever win against archrival Oklahoma, Earl found himself at the top of his game and truly in a position to bring the first-ever Heisman Trophy home to Texas. The next week, Earl rushed for 188 yards on 34 carries as the nation watched the 'Horns defeat the Arkansas Razorbacks. But, that week, Earl also displayed his receiving abilities. Taking a pass from quarterback McEachern, Earl dashed down the sideline, dodged Razorback defenders, and bulldozed a defensive back in the process. The referee called Earl down at the 1-yard line, but that play convinced sports fans all across the country that Earl Campbell was one of the most outstanding all-around athletes in the country.

The Longhorns won their next two games against SMU and Texas Tech. Ranked number one in the country, the 'Horns were determined to prove to everyone that they were the team to beat. Earl, too, was not about to let anything stand in his way...not even the flu! The night before their next match-up against the Houston Cougars, Earl complained of a stomachache and a fever. With a 104-degree fever, Earl was put to bed, where he spent the night shivering and sweating. The next morning, although his fever had lowered to 101, the team doctor insisted that he not play in the afternoon game. But Earl had come so far in his life and beaten the odds before. He had overcome poverty at a young age, hatred and racism in his schools, the heartache of losing his father when he was only 11, and of course, his hamstring injury the previous year. He wasn't about to let a little flu bug stop him from playing in this game.

Earl ran for 173 yards on 24 carries that day, scoring three touchdowns in the process. On his second touchdown run, as many longtime UT fans will remember, Earl barreled through the back of the end zone, knocking a standing Longhorn named Bevo, the team mascot, completely off his feet. [Earl's] performance in the Houston game prompted Akers to say, "Earl Campbell is the greatest football player I have ever seen, and Ann Campbell is the best coach there ever was!"

With the next two games, wins over TCU and Baylor, under their belts, it was now time to turn focus to the annual Thanksgiving Day battle between A&M and Texas. With the game being televised nationally, Earl knew he had to have a solid game against the Aggies' vicious defense if he wanted to have a shot at winning the Heisman. Akers pulled him over before the game and said, "You get out there and get me anything over 150 yards rushing...if you do this, I feel certain that the award will be yours." Akers, of course, could not guarantee his promise, but Earl respected the coach and did not want to disappoint him. And so Earl rushed for more than 220 yards that day and led his 'Horns in defeating their most hated rivals, the Aggies, 57–28.

Earl Campbell and the University of Texas had made promises to each other four years prior to this win. Earl had promised to give Texas his heart, soul, and best athletic and academic efforts while in Austin. And that he did. He brought the University of Texas back to the level of athletic dominance it had acquired for so many years, and in a time when cheating and dishonesty were running rampant in the collegiate ranks, Earl represented the type of integrity that Texas had worked so hard to achieve. Texas had also made promises to Earl, and it, too, had come through on its word: Royal, Coach Ken Dabbs—the man who had recruited Earl so vivaciously during his senior year, his long-time friend [Louis] Murillo, Akers, and many others had promised Earl and his mother, Ann, that they would take care of him and look out for his well-being. They had done that successfully.

Earl had grown from a young, naïve boy who had never ventured beyond the outskirts of East Texas into a well-respected man who had traveled across the country, learned to relate to many different types of people, and most importantly, he was now in a position to further his football career in the National Football League. He had also become part of a new family...the Texas Longhorn football family.

But with all that Earl had accomplished personally and athletically in the past four years, there was still one major goal that had eluded him...winning the Heisman Trophy.

1977

Each year, the Downtown Athletic Club of New York presents one award to the nation's most outstanding college football player. The winner of the award is chosen from all college football players that year and is voted on by sportswriters and former winners of the trophy after the season is over. This award is the most coveted award in college football and is known as the Heisman Trophy.

With 4,443 NCAA yards and 41 touchdowns in his career as a Longhorn, it was inevitable that Earl Campell was the top contender for the prestigious Heisman award. Campbell received many awards such as All-SWC for three years and was named to the Bob Hope All-American team for two consecutive years. But he never even dreamed that he would be named 1977's Heisman Trophy winner. Even with several titles under his belt, Earl still remained humble throughout his successes.

The year 1977 was successful for Earl, with an impressive 1,744 rushing yards, 800 of those being yards after contact or YAC. Despite these statistics, Earl was still not confident that he would be named as the Heisman Trophy winner.

It was the first week of December 1977 when Earl, his mother, Ann, close friends Henry and Nell Bell, Louis Murillo, Darrell Royal, Brad Shearer, and Rick Ingraham all traveled to New York for the presentation of the Heisman Trophy award. That year was the first year the Heisman Trophy award was presented in the style of the Academy Awards.

There were several sports awards given that night, with various appearances made by famous sports athletes such as Reggie Jackson and O. J. Simpson. The event was incredibly flashy and was televised nationwide.

It seemed as if the moment would never come. But finally Reggie Jackson took the stage to announce the winner of "the Best Running Back in the Nation." Earl hoped that his name would not be called for this award, as he thought it would take him out of the running for the Heisman.

Reggie then opened up the envelope and said, "And...the winner is...from the University of Texas, Earl Campbell!" The audience roared in cheer and applause, but Earl [stumbled] to the stage in shock. This wasn't what he had come to New York for. He muttered words of thanks into the microphone after he accepted the award. Brokenhearted, Earl headed backstage then attempted to find his way back to his seat. While backstage, a voice [said], "You better get back to your seat; there's still another important award to be given out." At that time Earl did not realize that that voice belonged to O. J. Simpson. As Earl slowly walked back to his seat in disappointment, Brad Shearer and Rick Ingraham began encouraging Earl.

Earl was not paying attention when Jay Berwanger said over the loud speaker, "And now, the moment we've been waiting for: The award for the most outstanding college football player in America goes to Earl Campbell." Before Earl knew it, he was being slapped on the back by his friends and was being hugged. He began to make his way up to the podium as the orchestra began playing "The Eyes of Texas." He was at a loss for words as he looked out over the audience and felt a chill go through his body as he clutched the bronze statue. He concluded his acceptance speech by saying, "I will represent what a Heisman Trophy winner should be. Thank you very much." With those words, Coach Royal instantly knew that all of Earl's hard work and dedication was because of one person, Ann Campbell, Earl's mother.

Kirk Bohls, *The Sporting News*

GOOD FELLA

Ricky Williams joined Earl Campbell as a Heisman winner in 1998. A month before that season started, Kirk Bohls wrote in The Sporting News *that the running back "is not only college football's best player, he is its finest ambassador."*

University of Texas running back Ricky Williams is predicted to be the best in the nation at his position in 1998. Williams had the option to enter the NFL in 1998, but opted to return for his senior season and make a run for the Heisman Trophy.

With his combination of ability, accessibility, and loyalty to his school, Ricky Williams is not only college football's best player, he is its finest ambassador

This just in: Ricky Williams has flaws. True, the prototypical All-American running back for Texas is the closest thing to perfection in pads. But those who know him best insist Williams does have a dark side.

For instance, sources who spoke only under the promise of anonymity say Williams has never met a bed he couldn't leave unmade. He has a soft side so big, he has seen *Beaches* several times, loves chick flicks, and once got busted by his two sisters for crying during *Old Yeller*.

There's more. Sister Nisey says when Ricky let loose "intimidating" screams at karate tournaments, she would burst out laughing at his falsetto voice. "He sounded like a little girl," she says.

He's so painfully shy he often makes his twin sister, Cassie, act like his girlfriend because he hates to say no when coeds ask him out. Roommate Chad Patmon says Williams is so ill at ease among strangers in social settings he literally clings to his best friend.

Ricky lost more bicycles than most kids have their entire childhood, absent-mindedly forgetting them at playgrounds. Sandy Williams had to scold Ricky more than once for finding his mother's secret hiding places for Christmas presents and devilishly revealing their contents to his sisters. A baseball card entrepreneur, he once tricked a neighborhood kid into a Mickey-Mantle-for-Marv-Throneberry type deal until the boy's parent threatened to call the police.

Stop Ricky Williams? Mom knew how, and it usually involved a paddle, a telephone wire, anything handy. He got his last spanking at age 15 after he packed the pockets of his Raiders jacket with enough king-size Snickers and gum to give him a month-long sugar high. "I got more spankings than anyone in the history of spankings," Ricky says, grinning widely.

His biggest vice is an obsession with PlayStation, which he'll play for hours.

And that's about where this dark chapter of the Williams dossier ends. It doesn't get any worse than this. Aside from this harmless stuff, Williams has been, and still is, a poster boy for sainthood.

The 21-year-old modern-day Tom Sawyer remains the model student-athlete who deems values that much of society has come to accept as anachronistic—things such as commitment and loyalty and honor—as more important than personal glory and personal banking accounts.

That he is still in school shouts about his impeccable character, which is part of the reason *The Sporting News* recognizes the nation's leading returning rusher as not only the best college football player in the country, but also the embodiment of what's great about college football.

Williams graced the covers of no fewer than eight preseason magazines this summer after a phenomenal junior season in which he rushed for 1,893 yards and scored 25 touchdowns—both NCAA highs—and finished fifth in the Heisman voting.

He's pretty good out of pads, too.

When Williams announced in early January he was rebuffing the salivating NFL and its millions and was returning to school for his senior season, Austin rejoiced. The citizens of Longhorn country all but brought out palm fronds, and even opponents were impressed with the magnitude of his decision.

"I admire him for coming back," Texas Tech coach Spike Dykes says. "I feel the same way about him as I do about Peyton Manning. You can wave all that money in front of their faces, but it takes a special type of person to grow up and decide he still wants to have some fun. He's been such a classy guy, he's a good role model for a lot of people."

Money doesn't remotely drive Williams, who would have signed an NFL deal worth about $20 million, including a signing bonus of at least $4 million, had he gone pro. He can remember washing windows and scrubbing tile Sunday mornings before Jack in the Box opened, and then being told not to spend his hard-earned dough in one place when he cashed his $4.95 paycheck at the bank.

This unassuming kid with the radical 'do and a rumbling running style reminiscent of Texas legend Earl Campbell said he's coming back because he simply likes college football. And all its trappings. The packed stadiums. The roar of the crowd. Cheerleaders, run-through lines, and Keith Jackson. He's still moved by the memory of the Darrell K Royal–Texas Memorial Stadium grandstand chanting "Stay, Ricky, stay" as he walked off the field after the Longhorns' last home game of 1997.

Oh, and he would like to break Tony Dorsett's all-time rushing mark, win the Heisman, and take the Longhorns to their third major bowl game in four seasons.

Williams is that rare selfless individual who puts contentment over cash, devotion over dividends. He's Manning with a stiff arm, a guy who trusted his instincts, realized what he had, and didn't want to give it up sooner than he had to.

"He's very goal-oriented," says his new coach, Mack Brown. "I think he wanted to leave with a better team. Four-and-seven really bothered him."

Brown wants to make sure nothing interferes with Williams's focus on his final season. That is exactly why he made an exception to his team rule and allowed Williams to keep his antiestablishment dreadlocks, which he has worn since 10th grade in honor of Bob Marley, his favorite musician.

In fact, during Williams's whirlwind celebrity tour since last season as the best running back of 1997, he was as overwhelmed by having his picture taken with Ziggy Marley, Bob's son, at Austin's La Zona Rosa hot spot as he was meeting childhood hero Tony Gwynn when Williams was inducted into San Diego's Hall of Champions in his hometown last December.

About that hair. Williams and the discipline-minded Brown, who likes long locks about as much as he does losing seasons, spoke at length about those trademark ringlets. The coach has instructed his players to wear their hair in a manner that would help them get jobs after school. "Ricky's not going to need a job," says Brown, who recognized that enforcing his rule with Williams would be to no one's benefit.

Williams likes the job he has. And no one works at his harder than this 6'0", 225-pound speed-bruiser with 7.5 percent body fat, four body piercings, and a Mighty Mouse tattoo. He led the nation in rushing with 172 yards a game and in scoring with 13.8 points per game, and poses the first legitimate threat to break Dorsett's all-time NCAA rushing mark of 6,082 yards. Those are just a few of the things that set him apart.

This is a college athlete who loves kids more than Barney does and spends as much time at elementary schools as a crossing guard. His genuine affection for youngsters so consumes Williams that he once almost missed a flight to an awards dinner because he had promised a kid he would come to his birthday party.

He rarely drinks. He freely signs autographs to the point of carpal tunnel syndrome. Two days after he declared his intention to return, he signed autographs for almost half of the 16,000 fans who attended the Kansas-Texas basketball game at Frank Erwin Center in Austin.

He's not too good to be true. He's better. "He always does things right," says Patmon, his best friend and a walk-on Longhorn defensive back.

He's forgiving. Last August he was arrested for a rolling stop by a campus policeman who was oblivious to Williams's identity and had trouble accepting the fact his driver's license belonged to Errick Williams, his given name. In the brief furor that followed, the officer was fired (and later rehired). Williams never said he wanted the man to lose his job.

He's humble. He has never spiked the ball or mouthed off to an opponent or a referee. He was stunned when Ryan Leaf, Peyton Manning, and Charles Woodson all praised him at a college football presentation in December. He later confided to a friend: "Tony Gwynn knows my name."

Gwynn is hardly alone. Williams is wildly popular. At Texas's final spring football game, he was mobbed afterward by children and adults of all ages in the record crowd of 21,000. As Williams retreated from the north end zone of the stadium after an hour-long autograph-signing session, the cluster around him gave the appearance of a mammoth centipede. "He looked like a rock star being escorted off stage," Texas football sports information director John Bianco says. "He's the only person I know who can say nothing and have charisma."

He's not the most ambitious student enrolled at Texas—he's a B and C student—but he desperately wants to get his degree and someday become an elementary school teacher. Kids ask to see his muscles and want to race him. It's adults who see him signing autographs and ask "Who are you?" who bug him.

He's considerate. During last year's miserable season, Williams would make regular Sunday visits to John Mackovic's office to cheer up his forlorn coach. After winning the Doak Walker Award as the nation's top running back, Williams has written more than 20 letters to Walker, who was paralyzed in a skiing accident last January.

Did we mention he's versatile? For the third-straight summer, he played in the Philadelphia Phillies' farm system and, despite struggling to hit the curveball, hit a career-best .283. However, he keeps those options open not out of a need for leverage with NFL general managers at the bargaining table, but out of a childhood love for the sport. He fully plans to play in the Phillies' farm chain again next spring before NFL training camp and says he could reach the majors in three years if he played year-round.

But he excels at football now. He's an attainable 1,928 yards shy of breaking Dorsett's 22-year-old record. Williams would have to average 175 yards a game to eclipse Dorsett and needs 289 yards to erase Earl Campbell's career mark of 4,443 yards at Texas. No one is betting against Williams.

This is a player off a 4–7 team who was honored as the Doak Walker winner in a ceremony in Orlando. He was so enthralled with the honor that on the flight back to Texas, he wouldn't take his eyes off a replica of the trophy that would be presented to him at a formal dinner in Dallas in February. An awards representative asked if he'd like to hold it. Williams held the statue in his lap the entire three-hour trip.

This is a modest person who shunned the millions that the NFL had to offer to stay in school—he was advised he would have gone between fourth and seventh in the draft. For now, Williams doesn't even plan to attend next year's NFL draft festivities in New York. "I'll stay home, a couple of high-fives...and go shopping."

Williams is not without ego, cloaked, though it is, under all that natural humility. He is driven by success but claims he isn't worried that he can't possibly match the grandiose expectations Longhorns faithful have for him. He realizes Texas fans will no longer be satisfied with mundane 100-yard games from a player who has six 200-yard games and who needs six more to replace Marcus Allen for the most in a career.

"Worrying is a waste of time," Williams says. "I don't really care what the fans want. Whatever they want, I'm going to want more."

He wants to win the Heisman. He wanted to win it last year, too, although he thought Leaf, who finished third, was most deserving. He was heartbroken when he wasn't even among the players invited to the award ceremony, but the truth is that he will have no regrets if he doesn't win the Heisman or break Dorsett's mark.

"If I break my leg and never play football again," he says, "it still wouldn't have been a mistake to come back."

Texas's poor season undoubtedly had much to do with the Heisman balloting. A porous defense that ranked 104th nationally against the run last season doesn't promise to improve that rapidly, and a still-unproven senior quarterback, Richard Walton, might not be able to force opponents to relax their concentration on Williams. A brutal schedule that includes trips to Nebraska, UCLA, Kansas State, and Texas Tech won't help a rebuilding team, either. Williams is the best player in the country, but he might not win the Heisman.

The last Heisman winner off a team with a losing record was Notre Dame's Paul Hornung, who edged Tennessee's Johnny Majors in 1956. Like Williams last year, a rugged running back out of Syracuse named Jim Brown finished fifth.

Williams is so intense about the upcoming season he cut short his baseball season and returned to Austin from Batavia, New York, in early July. But he did make giant strides toward becoming a more polished baseball player.

"I'm just more mature," he says. "All the guys hung out together, and were all real close. It was hard for me to leave."

For Ricky Williams, it always is.

Bill Minutaglio, *The Sporting News*

TEXAS TWO-STEP

Preceding the Vince Young era, the Longhorns were embroiled in a quarterback controversy that Mack Brown had to sort out. Who should start, Chris Simms or Major Applewhite? Bill Minutaglio tackled the controversy in The Sporting News.

The coach is too smart to call it a quarterback controversy—so the rest of the Lone Star State has obliged. Who will start for the Longhorns, Chris Simms or Major Applewhite? That's a call Mack Brown will make, but he could change his mind every week.

All around this inner-city football field, topped by a bristly crew-cut of grass, you can see ominous gray waves of 100-degree heat thrashing together. Look hard and you can see something else. Even though his face is mostly hidden inside his helmet, there is alarm registering with the deeply spiritual man wearing No. 11. He is locked inside the biggest quarterback controversy in the country—one deliberately set in motion by his coach—and right now it is as if he is seeing the past—and the future—all at once.

It's the first day of preseason workouts, and Texas quarterback Major Applewhite, who likes to talk about Moses, Abraham, and the inner conflicts of his biblical role models, is staring hard at Bo Scaife, one of the top tight ends in college football. Scaife had just dug the cleat of his left shoe into the hard, caked grass on UT's practice field, and though no one had hit him, it was as if the smothering heat and the unforgiving soil had reached up, vise-gripped his leg, and then given it a vicious twist. He had spun, his foot rooted to the ground, his mouth open with surprise, and then finally toppled over, tearing his anterior cruciate ligament. His season is over before it has begun. His coaches had said, before his injury, that Scaife would be an NFL pick one day.

The scene looks all too familiar to Applewhite.

A redshirt freshman starter in 1998, he was strafed by demanding Longhorns fans as just another forgettable, 6'1" servant for His Royal Heisman, Ricky Williams. Cherub-faced Applewhite—and what kind of name is Major Applewhite, anyway?—was under house arrest in chat rooms and newscasts: Too small, brainy but hockey-stick thin, he looked like a choir boy instead of a star from Catholic High in Baton Rouge, Louisiana.

But last year Applewhite shrugged it all off and went on to set 37 UT passing records. He seemed Super Glued in the pocket, even when the walls were crashing down around him. He could throw cross-field. He could improvise. And, after a game and talking to reporters from the voracious Texas media, he was as measured as Mike McCurry, who was unparalleled at explaining awkward moments inside the White House.

Last year it was hard to deny Applewhite—the most unlikely Co-Offensive Player of the Year in the Big 12. There were even whispers he could make a nice NFL player some day—whispers that abruptly turned into doubts when he ripped his anterior cruciate ligament in the Cotton Bowl against Arkansas.

Now, as he watches Scaife hobble away, the first thing Applewhite thinks about is what his own father told him after he blew out his knee: "What's the worst thing that can happen to you?"

His injured son, facing six months of rehab, said he didn't know.

"The worst thing that can happen is that you'll injure the same knee again," his father said.

Applewhite, who seeks nourishment from his family and his faith, agreed with his father.

But, of course, Applewhite's father hadn't seen the whole picture. There was something else, someone else—someone whom the coaches had lured to Austin to test Applewhite, to push him, to see if he would break.

And now that person is standing just a few yards away from Applewhite with the fallen Scaife doing the exact same thing—weighing his own past and future.

Chris Simms is a 6'5" sophomore quarterback, a Thoroughbred with the hungry eyes of Brett Favre. He's the one tossing the ball so high and so far that Longhorns receivers sometimes look like confused center fielders trying to find the orb as it plummets out of the sun. Simms, of course, is the son of Super Bowl MVP Phil Simms, and coming out of New Jersey, he was once one of the top recruits in the nation.

Chris Simms didn't grow up in the soul of the Lone Star State, but he could have—should have—because he looks like one of those toothy All-American cowboys from the land of Friday night lights, one of those rangy sons of a sod-buster who throws Roman candles up into the star-filled sky knowing full well that it will be another six on the board. He has dimples, sideline groupies, and an invisible halo that says "The Natural" hovering over his head.

Last year, with fans constantly searching the stands for glimpses of his famous father, Simms bucked and snorted in the stable. But the better Applewhite played, the less Simms was seen. There were nagging thoughts that he wanted out, that he felt he had made a mistake by picking Texas instead of Tennessee. He saw spot duty against Texas A&M, but only because Applewhite had a stomach virus. In practice he continued to hurt the hands of receivers, and a perception was quickly setting in cement.

Applewhite is the rocket scientist, and Simms is the flame thrower. Applewhite must rely on his brain and heart as he tries to peer over the line. Simms simply steps back and muscles the ball wherever he wants, whenever he wants.

Just like that, a Texas-sized quarterback controversy rolled across the state. Except, of course, don't call it a controversy—even though that's what Coach Mack Brown has deliberately, calculatedly set in motion. According to the Longhorns party line, it's...well...it's just a friendly competition in a year when all the expectations are crashing together in a state where football is equal parts religion and oxygen.

Not since the hallowed Darrell Royal era has there been so much hype, hustle, and hope brewing at Hut's hamburger emporium, Cisco's taco joint, Scholtz Bier Garten, or any of the other legendary Austin hangouts where people bleed orange and still can name everyone who turned out in formation in front of Earl Campbell or alongside Tommy Nobis.

Ranked number seven by *The Sporting News* heading into its season opener Saturday against Louisiana-Lafayette, Texas faces the Mother of All Expectation Years. "It's a healthy situation," deadpans defensive coordinator Carl Reese.

And, oh, by the way, Applewhite spent his summer getting his knee back to almost 100 percent, attending a football camp, and conferring with Peyton Manning and his famous father, Archie Manning. He spent virtually every evening watching film. He spent countless, lonely hours on stationary bikes. "I have a new passion for what I want to do. This is a different Major. This is a different moment," he says.

And, oh, by the way, over the summer Chris Simms put on 20 pounds of muscle, he talked to his father a lot, and he has been throwing so hard that he even broke a finger on the old man's hand when the two were playing catch. Now Phil Simms has to wear goofy, oversized winter mittens whenever they toss the ball.

And, oh, by the way, Chris Simms also decided to change his number this year.

It used to be No. 8.

Now it's No. 1.

"People think I am planting subliminal messages," says Simms with a grin as wicked as his passing arm. "No way."

And no way has it escaped the notice of fevered Longhorns numerologists that his rival's jersey just happens to have two number 1's stacked next to each other.

Let the games begin.

One quiet day, deep inside the sprawling, palatial UT football facility—a place that Mack Brown, when he arrived three years ago from North Carolina, had ordered to be turned into a ceaseless, shimmering shrine to every bit of UT football lore—Major Applewhite is stumped.

He is wondering if he should answer a question: Did he feel that, as the former starter, he was owed something? Did Applewhite, who had slaved anonymously through the Ricky Williams era, who never lashed out at the critics, who set all those records, think Brown owed him a longer look than usual?

Usually smooth with every media inquiry, he turns to a nearby university spokesman and asks for help in shaping an answer. "How would you answer that one?" begs Applewhite. "I don't know what to say."

For a brief, uncorked moment, Applewhite doesn't seem like the guy Reese says "is a competitor, I mean, if you played tiddlywinks with him, he's going to compete and scratch and try to find a way to beat you." His hands resting on the black brace wrapped around his reconstructed knee, he begins very, very slowly.

"I don't think I deserve preferential treatment, but I think that my experience and my past record have allowed me to be in the position where the coaches are going to have to give me a hard look," he says.

"I have seen too many big, strong, fast, stupid quarterbacks. And I have seen some very smart, wise, slow quarterbacks. But you have to combine a solid arm with solid feet with a solid mind and a tough mind, a smart mind. I don't think that height completes passes, and I don't want a quarterback out there that has a super-strong arm if he can't get past that comment. You have to know the game, beyond having an arm."

As he finishes, Applewhite, who spends his off hours visiting children in local hospitals, seems almost aghast—as if he realizes that when he's talking about height, about super-strong arms, it sure sounds as if he's talking about Chris Simms. He wants it known that he respects Simms, that he likes competition, that they roomed together on the road last year.

"It's work, work, work. We'll have time to rest when we die. My desire to work is bigger than ever before," says Applewhite, whom offensive coordinator Greg Davis describes as a potential offensive coordinator himself. "I honestly feel that it's the Lord's work refining me to do something special. I feel like he is refining me for a certain point in time," Applewhite said.

But even though Applewhite says he is weary from being asked about it, it's clear he has thought late into the night about keeping his starter's job, about his knee, about the way perceptions take root and never leave. He even invokes the name of one of the richest men in the world, former UT student Michael Dell: "I enjoy the compliment of being called brainy, but how good is it being brainy without any physical skills? How good would Michael Dell be over there in his dormitory in Austin if he didn't have the motherboards and some monitors and some things like that? He had to have the tools. When he had the tools, he developed them into a multibillion-dollar company."

When Chris Simms's father was locked in a New York death match with Jeff Hostetler for the starting quarterback gig with the Giants, Chris did something sneaky. There were polls in the local papers asking fans to pick the starter, and the younger Simms would call in 100 times a day, trying to tilt the outcome toward his father. "We had everyone calling in from our area," he remembers. "I really think I used to get more nervous for Dad's games than I do for my own games."

When Simms was told he was going to start as a freshman for his high school varsity team in New Jersey, his father pulled him aside. "There are a lot of people out there who will do anything to be a good football player," is all Phil Simms told his son.

Years later Chris Simms remembers that moment. "I heard what he was saying: Since I'm his son, and maybe spoiled a little, that I wouldn't work as hard at it. And I really took that personally. There were people coming out of rougher situations than I am, obviously. And I took that to heart. I will never forget it."

His father also has repeatedly said he will stay out of the UT spotlight, not wanting to pressure his son or Mack Brown. When he is in Austin, he wears a hat and sunglasses and does the whole incognito routine. Simms sees his father behaving like Pete Sampras's understated father—not Venus Williams's over-the-top father—at Wimbledon. "There is an art to what Sam Sampras did with Pete Sampras, and look where his son is," the younger Simms says.

Simms, like Applewhite, is weary of the competition talk—but completely, utterly aware of it and absorbed by it. He wants the team. He likes the fact that Reese says Simms "can throw the ball on a frozen rope. Anytime you have a taller quarterback, his vision is better from the pocket."

But, in the end, Simms wants to be recognized for his leadership skills. In other words: He wants to be number one, just like it says on his uniform.

"This year I want to be a leader," Simms says. "It's like an old-fashioned competition. It's like cowboys and Indians. Gunslingers."

It's no wonder Major Applewhite is drawn to running back Hodges Mitchell, the 5'7", 185-pounder from Dallas who constantly has "undersized" and "overachiever" penciled in next to his name.

"Those are the two words that drive me crazy," says Mitchell, one day after hitting the weights. "I see myself as a hard worker. Major is the same way. He takes hits and gets right back up. Chris, physically, is probably one of the best quarterback prospects I have ever seen. Major is more businesslike. Simms, he gets in the huddle, he is playing around, joking around while he is calling plays."

You hear it elsewhere on the team:

"Major is more of a thinker. He really knows the whole game; he knows what everybody is doing in the huddle," says Montrell Flowers, the Longhorns' deep threat. "Chris will probably get there later, but right now Major is the thinker and Chris is the athlete."

But mostly you hear the kind of thing that Longhorns' offensive lineman Antwan Kirk-Hughes says: "Most people in the nation would want to have two quarterbacks like that. Either one of them is number one."

Off campus, in his Hill Country home, Darrell Royal has been watching it all like Obi-Wan Kenobi. Previous coaches had exiled Royal from UT, but when Brown moved to Austin from North Carolina, one of the first people he called was the local legend. Brown set him up with an office and made sure Royal, Earl Campbell, and anybody else from the storied past were welcome whenever they wanted—something that has turned out quite handy in keeping fans, alumni, recruits, and boosters happy. And when Royal arrived back on campus he was still, after all these years, as sly as a wink from his best pal Willie Nelson.

"Controversy? I am not aware of any controversy," he says. "Maybe between mamas."

After a while, Royal concedes a bit. "They are both going to be playing," he says. "The question is who is going to be the starter. I talked to Major personally, and he said (his knee) was fine. Now that's a boy talking to you. But if anyone can handle it, Major can."

James Street, the former UT star quarterback, has less reason to be so diplomatic. "Any way you want to look at it, it has got to be a delicate situation," he says. "One is taller, throws the ball a lot harder—although Applewhite throws the long pass great. He does not have the zip on the ball on the shorter passes that Simms does. Simms will come in, and you will see a ball go through a kid's hands. Sometimes Simms throws the short pass harder than he probably needs."

The quarterback shootout has turned into the kind of cinematic battle that has lured fans and media from coast to coast, the kind of headline-dominating story Brown has craved since those days when he was constantly being overshadowed by Dean Smith's Tar Heels basketball program.

"In Texas there is almost a religious fever that you've got to be good, and Mack has tapped into that," marvels Davis, who, as offensive coordinator, must oversee the competition where it matters most—in the locker room and on the practice field.

"They (Simms and Applewhite) are probably more similar than the average fan would want them to be," says Davis, who patterns the UT offense after the Buffalo Bills'. "The key word in dealing with these two kids is trust. They have to trust Mack and I in our decision-making, they have to trust that we are doing what's right for the team. And we have to trust them, when they go into the locker room or go to the media, that they impart the same line."

From afar, Ricky Williams knows better than most what's going on at UT. He knows that Brown, dating back to his days at Carolina, always has revered the concept of creating battles for positions. In Brown's confident, chess-playing mind, no one permanently owns a position: "That's how it is with Coach Brown," Williams says. "It's not really your position. Every year, at every position, it's going to be like that."

Somewhere on the Texas campus, right now, Mack Brown is chuckling. He has what analysts say is a very friendly schedule. He is sitting on top of the world with two studs he can put at the helm of a wide-open, West Coast–style, quarterback-friendly offense that Reese has playfully dubbed "basketball on grass."

When he's asked about those unyielding expectations for his program, he smiles and tends to agree with Davis, who says the team is the deepest it has been in years at offensive line, running back...and, oh yes, quarterback.

Right now betting money is on Simms being the starter. But in Brown's world without nostalgia, the man who protects the ball the best is the one who will play more. Brown doesn't play favorites; he plays the people who are delivering that week, that day, that very minute. He may wait until Saturday morning to name his starting quarterback against Louisiana-Lafayette. And depending on what happens then, he may wait another seven days to name his starter for game two. And so on.

Truth be told, Brown likes this war he has set in motion. It has reporters eating out of his hand, it is selling thousands of season tickets, it has people clamoring to see his nimble recruiting handiwork—it even has people lining up to see the way he got his wife to do the interior decorating at the football facility, with the Heisman trophies on display, the miles of orange paint, the authentic Longhorn heads planted on the walls, the museum-style "memorial lockers" for Campbell and all the other stalwarts plunked down in the middle of the locker room.

"You know, I was standing out there on the sidelines today, and I said to myself: 'Who in America has got two guys that can stand out here and play like these two?'" a beaming Brown says one afternoon after practice. He is relaxing in a golf cart and watching Simms and Applewhite being swarmed by autograph hounds and reporters.

"Is this a great country or what?" responds someone sitting nearby.

"Oh, you bet it is," laughs Brown, his face filled with merry mischief— as if he is watching the curtain go up on Mack's Midsummer Night's Dream. Now he can see for himself exactly what happens when you have orchestrated a big-time football controversy deep in the heart of the Lone Star State.

Tom Buckley, *Horns Illustrated*

BOYS TO MEN

All-Americans Cedric Benson and Derrick Johnson followed similar, but not easy, paths to Texas as related in this story from Horns Illustrated.

Dwight Johnson knew that when the bell tolled at St. Paul's Episcopal Church in Waco, it was probably tolling for him. On those Sunday mornings, when he was all of nine, Dwight, a future NFL defensive tackle with the Philadelphia Eagles and New York Giants, had drawn what would be his toughest Sunday assignment: trying to control his three-year-old brother, Derrick, during the two-hour church service.

"He was a hyper little joker," Dwight laughs, "crawling over the pews, under the pews, ringing the church bell—right during the preaching. He couldn't stay still. My mama was in the choir, and I'd look up and see her gritting her teeth. I could read her lips, too. Someone was headed for a whooping."

Such was the curse of being the older brother charged with piloting his spirited younger sibling. Dwight learned to take the heat.

Like the time a bored Derrick disregarded his mother's wishes and, while Beverly Johnson was at work, began taking apart the rock garden in the front yard, tossing the rocks a distance, then tossing them back. Except one time he underestimated his strength and hurled a boulder right through the glass front door. "My mom was always telling me, 'Don't touch the rocks,'" Derrick recalls. "I was scared." So scared, in fact, that when Dwight and older brother Dwayne raced to the scene, they found their brother screaming and crying. They knew what they had to do. "When I got home," Beverly says, "they covered for Derrick. They took the blame."

His mother wasn't the only authority figure young Derrick feared: he was terrified of his Pop Warner football coach, too. "I'd be crying because I didn't want to face him," Johnson says. "He was always hollering. But Mama would put some tough love on me, saying, 'Get out of the car; stop acting like a sissy.' Every year after that, I didn't want to go back. I was weak when it came to the coach."

His brothers decided to toughen him up, organizing Friday night boxing matches in their front yard, pitting their brother against older neighborhood kids. Once they taught the right-handed Derrick to stop swinging only with his left, he began winning his matches. Then they'd take him to a field nearby and run him through a series of intense tackling and running drills—just the three of them. "They'd line up side by side and tell me to run between them," Johnson says of his imposing brothers, "or they'd make me try and tackle them." The tasks proved nearly impossible for the baby of the family, but the lessons weren't lost on the future linebacker. "They taught me what I needed to do," Johnson says.

Meanwhile, across the state in Midland, Cedric Benson was fretting over another broken lamp. Or perhaps a dish. Or table top. Confined to the house while his mother, Jackqueline, was at work, the young Benson served both as caretaker to his younger brother, Dominic, and daily activities coordinator. "We couldn't go outside until Mom got home," Benson recalls, "so we'd have to entertain ourselves inside all day, every day." To keep his brother occupied, Benson turned the living room into a makeshift track meet, then later transformed the same room into a baseball diamond. "We broke a lot of stuff," Benson smiles. "I recall some anxiety when Mom was on her way home." Still, he accepted his role. "It was just the three of us, so I was always trying to make things easier on my mom."

When the two brothers ventured outdoors, Benson kept a close eye on Dominic. "I always had to stay near Cedric," Dominic recalls. "He made sure to keep me out of trouble." Still, Benson acknowledges he had to learn from his mistakes—like the time he thought playing hide-and-seek in a junkyard at night was a good idea. "I tripped, fell on a pipe, and passed out," he says. "I was pretty quiet, I guess, so they all thought I was just a great player. Later, I thought to myself, 'What are you doing running around at night with your brother in a junkyard?'"

John Parchman, Benson's high school coach at Midland Lee, recalls conversations with Benson about the responsibilities that came with being a big brother and surrogate father. "He didn't necessarily want that role," Parchman says. "I can almost see him sighing when he thinks about it—a big sigh." At night, after a long day of looking after his brother, he'd play by himself, assembling his marbles on the floor of his room like two football teams.

"My childhood," Benson says, "flew by."

Derrick Johnson and Cedric Benson were born a little over a month apart in 1982—Johnson in Central Texas, Benson in West Texas. They grew up in single-parent homes marked by discipline and sacrifice—and with mothers intent on keeping them away from the dangers that even their best friends were succumbing to. "There was nothing to do after dark," Beverly Johnson says, "but get in trouble." Johnson wasn't allowed to spend the night at anyone's house and rarely was allowed at parties; Benson had a 10:00 PM curfew—extended to midnight on weekends when he was an upperclassman—and if he wasn't home by then, he was required to call his mother to say he was on the way. He always did.

Johnson shared a room with his two brothers in the small, white-brick house in Waco; Benson and younger brother Dominic slept in bunk beds—Benson on top—in their two-bedroom home on Mineola Street in Midland. Both were expected to carry their weight around the house, which meant completing a seemingly never-ending list of chores. When neighborhood kids would laugh at Johnson because he was spending his weekends working—trimming bushes, washing walls, cutting grass, painting, working in the garden, taking out the trash—his mother would tell him, "You'll appreciate me later." Benson, for his part, saw his heavy workload as a necessary part of his role as mother's helper. "We made sure the house was clean and organized all the time," Benson recalls. "It was a struggle, but my mom never showed it. She was able to raise us, put clothes on us, feed us. She didn't need anybody else."

Johnson learned of his mother's humble beginnings—how she grew up in East Texas with 20 brothers and sisters, how they picked cotton and took turns sending each other to college. "Mom," he'd ask whenever he needed something, "do you have enough money to get me this?"

Benson learned to live with hand-me-downs: "I remember telling myself, 'I'm not gonna ask for anything else. I'm gonna be satisfied.' I started playing football in sixth grade," he says, chuckling, "and there comes a point when all you really care about is what you're gonna wear—how you need to get these cleats, these gloves, these wrist-bands. All my equipment came second-hand from my cousin."

Waco and Midland were worlds removed but beset by the same sorts of problems—drugs, gang violence, high dropout rates—that every parent fears. "There were lots of temptations in Waco," Johnson says. "Being a smaller city, there's not much there to do. So many of my friends—good friends—are dead...or in jail...or just dropped out and aren't doing anything now." Benson, determined to make things easier on his mother by avoiding any such shenanigans, would sign himself up for after-school programs. "Most kids would let their parents sign them up, I guess," he says, "but I understood what my mom was going through. I saw what it was like on the better side of town—the two-parent homes—but I just decided, 'This is the way it is for me.'"

Football provided further incentive to walk the straight path. "I had brothers and cousins in front of me who went to college and received scholarships because of football," Johnson says. "I wasn't about to mess that up." Neither was Benson, who recognized early on that his on-field talent could be his ticket out. "A lot of my friends got in trouble and didn't make it out," Benson says, "or are still trying to make it out. I knew if I got in trouble, I couldn't play football anymore. And I wanted to play."

Soon, these two physically gifted athletes from different parts of Texas would share more than the similarities in their upbringings: they'd be among the finest high school football players in the state—and the nation—blessed with an opportunity to go almost anywhere in the country to play college football.

They wouldn't venture far.

"Derrick was a very happy kid," Beverly Johnson says of her youngest child. Unlike his older brothers, though, he was also thin as a rail. "I used to look at him," Beverly says, "and think, 'Why is he so little—so much smaller than my other boys?'" That answer came, in part, when Johnson was older and his brothers fessed up. "They told me that whenever I left the table, they'd eat Derrick's food for him. They felt sorry for him, so they were his garbage disposal."

It's a wonder, given his preferred diet of candy and pizza, that Johnson possessed the energy he did. He was so hyper, in fact, that his mother would give him coffee on the drive in to school each morning to calm him. "It's the only thing that worked," she laughs. "As long as Derrick had his morning coffee, he'd be okay." That didn't necessarily keep him still in the classroom, though, and his teachers would send notes home as evidence. And Johnson did what any fearful child might do: he hid them—in places he thought no one would ever look, like the stereo or the Bible. "I'd always find them, of course," Beverly says, "and I'd call him and tell him to collect all the notes and bring them to me. His eyes would get real big, and he'd say, 'But Mama?' Then he'd start crying."

Johnson showed no such fear out of doors. At age four, he got on a bike for the first time and rode away, making sure to look back and grin at his dumbfounded brothers, who'd struggled in their early bike-riding attempts. Then he fell off—and got right back on. He jumped curbs with skateboards, swung through trees with abandon, and ran through trash cans he'd set up to block him.

He was a man of action—not of words.

"Being the baby," Johnson says, "I learned to be quiet. I had older brothers, an older sister, plenty of cousins. I let everyone else do the talking. I listened to them." He watched them, too, and learned from them—not merely what to do, but what not to do. "He didn't want to make some of the mistakes we did," Dwight says. "He had a vision of how to conduct himself from observing us. He was always a good kid—never a party kid, never hung with the wrong crowd."

Still, he was placed in a tough position when many of his friends began using drugs. "I didn't speak up," Johnson says. "I was really shy. It was more like, 'Maybe they'll stop if they see me not doing it.' That's the one thing I'd do differently if I could go back. My actions weren't enough."

Even on the football field, he wouldn't say a word, though he made a lot of noise. A *Parade* All-American at Waco High, Johnson collected 170 tackles, six sacks, and two interceptions as a senior, earning first-team all-state honors. In one game alone, versus John Tyler High School, he forced four fumbles and registered 30 tackles. He also jotted something down in a notebook, which he placed in a bottom drawer and vowed never to look at again until he was sure it was true: "Best Linebacker in the Nation," it reads. Last year, he was one of three finalists for the Butkus Award, given to the nation's top linebacker; this year he's the preseason favorite. The notebook awaits.

"I've had the good fortune of working with a lot of very talented linebackers in the NFL—Pro Bowl players," UT defensive coordinator Greg Robinson says. "I'd like to think Derrick doesn't take a back seat to any of them. He's got the whole package: great speed, quickness, instincts. He can run, he can bend, he can drop his weight to change direction and redirect. He's very gifted."

And he's found his voice. While he was a quiet force his freshman and sophomore campaigns at Texas—he was *The Sporting News'* National Freshman of the Year and a Butkus Award semifinalist as a sophomore—Johnson surprised himself last season with his new-found vocal presence. "I talked more than I thought I would," he says, "trying to motivate my teammates. It was fun to see the guys' reaction." This spring, he was more comfortable in his role as vocal leader. "He's leading naturally," Robinson says. "I didn't put that on him. He doesn't have a problem turning to another player and letting them know how strongly he feels. And I don't think anyone has a problem hearing that from him. They respect him so much; they buy into him."

Even Johnson's family is taken aback by his transformation. After classes ended this spring, Johnson returned home to speak to middle schoolers where his sister, Daphanie, teaches. "She was so impressed with his maturity," Beverly says. "She said to me, 'Did Derrick say that?'" Mama had her moment, too. There was a time when Johnson depended on Beverly, a teacher, to help him with his school speeches; but last year, at the Butkus Award ceremony, Johnson wrote and delivered his own speech, alerting the audience beforehand that his mother was in the crowd and would be grading him on his performance. "I made sure to work her into the speech," Johnson smiles, "so she liked it." And his grade? "B plus," Beverly laughs. "I told him, 'Next year, you'll win the award and get an A plus.'"

"His first year at college," Dwight recalls, "he was immature—he had to learn to live alone, learn to get his grades up, needed me to tell him, 'You have to be fierce about football and grades.' Now, I feel like I'm talking to a man."

Though Cedric Benson began playing football for a local Midland team, the Colts, in sixth grade—with Benson, the previously unheralded team won the league's Super Bowl—it wasn't until his sophomore year at Midland Lee that he discovered his true inspiration. "Mom," he announced one day, "I want to be just like Ricky Williams." Recognizing the seriousness of intent in her son's eyes, Jackqueline soon established an important ground rule: no dreadlocks until after Benson had graduated. "He wore braids throughout high school," she recalls, "but the day after he graduated, he went out and got dreadlocks, and he's worn them ever since."

At the time, Benson wasn't paying much attention to the college game—he was too busy annihilating high school opponents—but once his cousin told him about Williams, he went out, bought some magazines, and became infatuated. "I had this picture of him in my mind—the way he carried himself on the field," Benson says. "I tried to walk like him, run like him. Of course I didn't quite have his moves," he smiles, "but after the whistle blew, I was Ricky Williams."

At Midland Lee, Benson could easily have been mistaken for the former Heisman Trophy winner. "Surely, he's the best at carrying the football of anyone I've ever coached," Midland Lee's John Parchman says. "And he may be the best I've ever seen."

All the folks in West Texas know the Benson legacy—how he was a three-time Texas 5A Offensive Player of the Year, how he rushed for more yards than any player in 5A history, how he led Midland Lee to a 43–3 record and three consecutive 5A State Championships (only the fourth team in state history to win three straight titles). He was a *Parade* All-American, *USA Today*'s Texas Player of the Year, and a finalist for the High School Heisman.

And he wanted nothing to do with the spotlight.

But when he scored five touchdowns in the state title game as a sophomore, the bright lights found him. "He came in at 165–70 pounds and left as a 200-pound senior," Parchman says. "But more than that, he matured as a man. Understand that everyone treated him as a full-grown man since he was a sophomore, but we never lost sight of the fact that he was a kid. He still had growing to do. He'd served as a father figure at home, but he hadn't been fathered himself. And he needed to be fathered."

Parchman made sure Benson took—or retook—all the right classes, finished his homework, and stayed out of trouble by providing the kind of counsel every teenage boy requires. "He needed someone to tell him, 'Dumb ass, you can't do that,'" Parchman says. "He needed that sort of foundation." After struggling during one game, an exasperated Benson exclaimed to his coach, "I can't do it by myself," to which Parchman responded, "Why not? The great ones can." Benson stormed away, then returned shortly thereafter. "You're right," he told Parchman. "Give me the ball."

During one state championship game in Austin, after Lee had run a successful sweep to the left, Benson caught Parchman's attention on the sidelines. "He made this motion with his arm as if to say, 'Run the play again,'" Parchman recalls. "We ran it six times in a row—he scored the sixth time. When he came over to the sidelines, his eyes were real big, and he said, 'I didn't know you'd run it six times in a row!' And I said, 'Heck, I didn't know it would take you six times to score!' He gave me that big smile of his, and we both just laughed and laughed."

Thanks to the influence of Ricky Williams, Benson's recruiting process was abbreviated. He always knew where he'd end up, and rumors that he was considering Oklahoma late in the game were, he says, patently false. "I never even considered OU," he says. "I wanted to stay in Texas. I'm Texas-born, and there's such great fan support here." During his lone recruiting visit to Austin, he made sure to call Parchman. "He'd tell me where he was eating," Parchman laughs. "One night he said, 'I ate at some lady's steakhouse. The food was pretty good.' I said, 'Do you mean Ruth's Chris?' and he said, 'Yeah, she's the one.'"

Four years later, Benson is poised to become the first running back in school history to rush for more than 1,000 yards each of his four seasons at Texas—something even former Heisman winners Earl Campbell and Williams didn't accomplish.

He's always been quiet—never outspoken, always someone who'd think before he spoke, if he spoke at all. "He lets others do the talking," his mother, Jackqueline, says, "and he does the thinking." He's perceived inaccurately, he says—as cocky and aloof—because he's quiet, especially around people he doesn't know. "I'm pretty simple," he says. "I'm from West Texas; that's where I was raised. When I'm joking or being sarcastic, I don't usually smile, so it's hard for people to get where I'm coming from." He's bothered by the negative press—when it seems, he says, that everyone is looking down on him. "I deal with it myself," he sighs. "I stay in my head. That's a lot of heat." But it's not pressure. "Pressure," Benson says, "is having your number called when you're behind in a game and your team needs you to get a first down."

Pressure may also be meeting your idol for the first time, something that happened to Benson during his freshman season. "I didn't know what to say, what to do," Benson says of meeting Ricky Williams. "You want to say all the right things, do all the right things." After the game, Benson called his mother. "Mom!" he exclaimed. "I met Ricky! He's nothing like I thought he'd be. He's really down-to-earth—just like me."

It was only fitting, perhaps, that following their junior seasons, Texas's two preseason All-Americans were faced with the same potentially life-altering decision: whether or not to turn pro. Johnson, who chose Texas over Oklahoma four years ago because of the team's family atmosphere—"Everyone here," he says, "seemed to take you in a little more"—knew he wasn't ready. "I still needed to learn," he says, "to spend more time in the film room, to learn my assignments better, to be a vocal leader." The promise of NFL riches didn't tempt him. "Mom," he told Beverly, "the money doesn't mean anything to me. I need to grow up more." Dwight seconded his younger brother's decision. "I told him, 'There are sharks out there, and they're gonna be coming at you.' He's an innocent kid; he's just a boy who likes to play football. I'm not sure he's ready for what's going to happen."

But he's ready to take charge of the Longhorn defense. "He's begun to assess his commitment," Robinson says. "I can just see him thinking, 'I stayed. Why? I know why.' And now he's feeling his commitment."

Offensive coordinator Greg Davis has noticed the same qualities in Benson, who took the additional step of giving up professional baseball—something Ricky Williams also did before his senior season. "He's a great example for the younger guys because of his work ethic," says Davis.

Like Johnson, Benson isn't preoccupied with his eventual payday. "I won't do much with the money," he says. "I'll definitely take care of my mom and put money away for my brother to go to school." He elected to stay, he says, because he wants to lead Texas to a national title. "Championships," he says, "are all we talk about where I'm from." His goals for this season are simple: rush for 2,000 yards and play in the national title game in Miami come January. "Actually, let me adjust that," he says. "My goal is to make it to Miami, because if we make it, I'm pretty sure I'll have 2,000 yards." And if that happens, Benson won't be the only one smiling.

Eric Neel, *ESPN the Magazine*

KEEPER

Eric Neel wrote this revealing feature on Vince Young in the December 5, 2005, edition of ESPN the Magazine, *one month before the quarterback's heroics in the Rose Bowl.*

Vince Young hums. Just before every opening kickoff, standing alone behind the bench, he beat-boxes "June 27th," the classic slow-ride joint by fellow Houstonian DJ Screw. He bobs his head a bit and puts a subtle wiggle through his 6'5", 233-pound frame. All flow, no hustle. "I'm loose," he says of these moments. "I get that drive, that beat, and I'm dancing before it's even game time."

He keeps the groove once the game is on. It's third and 10 on his own 20. The Longhorns are down 28–12 to start the third quarter at Oklahoma State. The junior quarterback takes a deep drop but sees covered wideouts everywhere, so he quickly steps up and glides between his blockers. Then it's a feint left and a step to the right, a little something he calls his Texas two-step, and he's into free space. Cowboys safety Donovan Woods looks to bottle him at the line of scrimmage, but Young sells him a pump fake so funky it launches Woods into midair. Ten seconds, 35 strides, and 80 yards down the sideline later, [Young's] in the end zone, and Texas is on its way to 35 unanswered points. "He's got so many moves," says tackle Justin Blalock. "He's like a kid out there, having fun."

And it's hard to imagine anyone in college football having more of it than Vince Young these days. He's first among three equals in this season's Heisman race; he's 27–2 for his career; and he and his boys are undefeated, ranked second, and headed for a Rose Bowl showdown with USC.

The coach swears by him. "He's the best quarterback in the country," says Mack Brown. "And the bigger the scene, the better he likes it." The fans idolize him. They come out by the thousands to get his autograph on signing days. "He's embraced here like no one I've ever seen," Brown says. And teammates adore him. "The guy is magnetic," says tight end David Thomas. "You're just drawn to him."

In the first team meeting after last season's 38–37 Rose Bowl win over Michigan, Young set a tone for the future. The mood was loud and light when he walked to the front of the room. Like a father setting sons right, he made everyone sit up, take their hats off, and listen to what the coaches had to say. The Rose Bowl was big but just a beginning, Young told them. "I won't accept what's good right now," he remembers saying. "I want us to achieve greatness." He continued to challenge his teammates over the summer, with a note on the locker room bulletin board: "If you want to beat Ohio State, meet me here every night at 7:00 PM for seven-on-seven." The turnout was faithful and focused. Many nights saw full 11-on-11 scrimmages.

But if Young is team leader, he's also one of the boys. He's serious and dedicated but never tight. Young punches a lineman in the shoulder, whispers to a corner that he'll never be able to cover the wideout coming to town this weekend, sings and shouts in the middle of practice—a little Al Green, a little rumble-young-man-rumble Cassius Clay.

"He's always dancing around, messing with somebody," Thomas says. "Just keeping things light." Walk-ons and freshmen get grief the same as his closest friends. "He makes everyone feel comfortable," Thomas continues in earnest appreciation. "We all feel like we're a part of things."

His teammates catalog favorite Vince Young moments. For Blalock, it's the fourth touchdown run in the Rose Bowl. For Thomas, it's Young stepping into the huddle and predicting a game-clinching score in the last minutes at Ohio State. They're just waiting for the day their kids and grandkids ask them what it was like to play with the immortal Vince Young.

Some quarterbacks are forged in the pressure of a collapsing pocket or the fire of a two-minute drill. [Young's] career was first tempered with a little help from a pair of handcuffs and a rake.

There was a gang fight at Dowling Middle School in Houston's Hiram Clarke neighborhood eight years ago, and by the end of it, Young was wearing bracelets and catching the business end of his mother's rage. "She was in my face," he says, "telling me I was going to end up dead or in jail."

Felicia Young—who worked long hours as a home health aide but also drank and lit up a joint some—had never really connected with her boy. "For a while, I wasn't really being much of a mother to my kids," she admits. But that changed on that spring day: "I had to put my foot down. The stakes were too high."

She told Vince that if he didn't change, he'd end up like his father, Vincent, who has moved in and out of jail like the place was offering Marriott Rewards points. She put Vince to work in the family's front yard, pulling leaves into piles, then scattered them so he could do it all over again. It gave him time to think about what his mother had said, about where his father was, about guys he'd seen who'd wasted their chances. "Some better athletes than me, guys who should be in the league right now," he says. And about paths and choices. "I saw the direction I was going, and I knew I needed to go another way," he says. "Those leaves got me right."

Nearly a decade later, Young's teammates chuckle when they talk about his determination. "I know it sounds cliché," Blalock says. "But the guy's will is incredible. He comes through. He won't let us lose." No kidding. In the past three seasons, Young has pulled off eight second-half comeback victories. Coach Brown is emphatic: "He's a tough sucker."

That toughness is written all over his right arm. Young pulls up his sleeve to reveal an elaborate tattoo of intertwined roses on his bicep. The flowers represent the women in his family. He gently rubs his fingers over the ink, as if touching a holy symbol. "I wanted to show how much I appreciate them," he whispers. Inspired by Vince's efforts to straighten up, and led by a neighborhood pastor who told her she'd be blessed through her son, Felicia became a born-again Christian seven years ago. She and her mother Bonnie have kept an especially tight ship since then, steering Vince from trouble and toward his promise. His older sisters, Lakesha and Vintrisa, were extra sets of eyes—and wagging fingers. When they married, each asked Vince to walk her down the aisle.

"A house full of women is a powerful thing," Felicia says with a laugh. "We intimidated him." Vince remembers it more charitably. "They wouldn't let me fall back," he says. "They wanted me to be different from my father, and different from so many of the men around us." So he carries them on every scramble, every follow-through, keeping the family close at hand. As they are his shield, so is he theirs. "I learned a lot of things on my own," Young says. "I remember going around locking the doors at night, knowing I was the protector for the women in our house. I grew up quick."

And strong and smart. Take the third quarter at home against Texas Tech. He steps to the line on third and five. The play call from coordinator Greg Davis features a short crossing route, but Young sees single coverage on wideout Billy Pittman. He audibles a go-route. Bam, a 75-yard backbreaker. "That's the fourth time this season he's checked down at the line and gotten a touchdown out of it," Davis says. "He's a very mature quarterback."

Man-against-boys mature. Since the Rose Bowl, when he ran through, over, and around the Wolverine defense for four hit-the-TiVo TDs (he threw for another), it's been clear Young is playing a different game. That night, Michigan head coach Lloyd Carr called him "the finest athlete I've ever been on the field with as a quarterback." But Davis, who has seen Young practice calls and cadences in front of a full-length mirror, knows it's more than athleticism. "Vince has worked hard at being a complete quarterback," he says. "The game has slowed down for him now. He's beyond the thought process. He's running through progressions, making decisions without dwelling on the steps."

Forget the steps. What about the motion? Well, Young's delivery comes out somewhere between putting a shot and skipping rocks on a pond. It's the one part of his skill set that isn't pretty, and exactly the sort of thing that raises questions about future prospects. "He's not the prototype," agrees Davis. "Neither is Philip Rivers, and neither was Bernie Kosar." Kosar with wheels? That works.

"I'm a quarterback," Young says simply. And it's hard to argue. He has a 169.8 passing efficiency rating through 10 games, second only to the 172.5 of UCLA's Drew Olson, and he has rushed for 774 yards, behind Missouri QB Brad Smith, who has 1,080. Texas has scored 40-plus points nine times. Brown is like most big-time college coaches, cautious and politic, but not when the subject is Young. "He'll be one of the great pro quarterbacks we've ever seen play," he says. "He'll be in the Hall of Fame."

Young thinks about the next level, about making his mark. He reclines in a high-backed swivel chair in the Longhorns' sports information office and looks off into the upper corner of the room, trying to find a window on the future. "I have goals," he says. "I want to someday be in the same position as John Elway, Joe Montana, Steve Young." Steve McNair, an old friend of Vince's uncle Ivory from their days at Alcorn State, has been a friend and mentor to Vince for five years, and he can see Young taking his place in the roll call. "Vince has what the league demands now, with the sophisticated defenses we see," McNair says. "You need the ability to run and the ability to beat teams with your arm. He has both pieces, the way Michael Vick and Donovan McNabb do."

Young recently said he's returning to Texas for a senior season, but outside of Austin, the news was met with a healthy dose of "we'll see." If Texas wins out, if Young wins the Heisman, the pressure to go pro will be intense. What's left to prove? Why risk an injury? Why wait to show what you can do?

Funny you should ask. "College is the best time of your life," Matt Leinart has said. "You live with your friends, just hang out, and have fun." Young feels that. He is the locker-room DJ, spinning 50 Cent and Chamillionaire, with a little Garth Brooks thrown in for his country-loving pal Thomas. He meets with friends from the team every Tuesday night for steaks. He goes head-to-head on the Xbox—NCAA Football 06—with his roommate, junior running back Selvin Young. He dances on the bus and cuts up on the practice field. "It's real fun right now," he says. "The team is a team. We're tight."

But Young isn't Leinart. There's much more to playing quarterback at UT for Young than the limelight and the good times. "I think being quarterback of this team is what God put me on earth for," he says. Ask him about his favorite moments from the season, and he might begin with the time a group of moms were lined up in the tunnel near the field and asked Felicia to lead them in prayer. Young's phone rings every morning; it's Felicia reciting a verse from her daily devotional reading. "I want him to know the Lord's work starts early," she says. Watching his mother's transformation has had a profound effect on Young. Her commitment has shadowed and now reinforces his own. "We look at each other now, me on the field and her in the stands, and we smile," Young says. "We know where we've been, what we've been through."

The same goes for Young's relationship with his coaches. After a narrow win over Missouri last year, and after weeks of trying and failing to fine-tune his motion, Young sat down with Davis and Brown, who told him to forget the motion and just play. "It was a key moment," Brown says. "I think he heard that as, 'We like you. We believe in you. We trust you.'" Late in the Missouri game this year, Davis called down to the sideline from his perch above the field to say "good job" and to sit his quarterback down for the rest of the game. "I love you, Coach," Young said back into the phone. "I love you, too," Davis replied, startled and touched by the exchange. Trust and love. There it is. The stuff you look for. "My coaches, my uncles, that's been everything to me," Young says. "Having guys like that around, looking at the things they do as men, I eat it up."

Young's 27–2 mark is one win shy of Bobby Layne's school record.

Young better get his fill of fun and fellowship while he can. "It's different in the pros," says McNair, who talks on the phone with Young a couple of times a week. "It's all business once you come out." Young doesn't shrink from that. And no decision has been made. "It depends on the season, then I'll sit down with my mother," he says, half under his breath, as if he hopes the decision will go away if he doesn't speak of it. "Right now, I'm just playing."

He's got game, statements to make, and a tattoo full of family to shoulder. "We've struggled," he says. "There were times we'd wear the same shoes for years, you know?" But don't assume he's feeding you a line when he says he's coming back. His memories drive him, but they make him want to linger, too. This time, this place, is home.

As Young walks out of the athletics office on a sunny fall day, a call comes in. A local reporter is petitioning sports information director John Bianco to interview Young about the Heisman. "Nah, it's not time for that," Young tells Bianco. "That can wait." He disappears into his black Chevy Tahoe and rolls down the window. The heavy bass of Houston hip-hop rises up out of the speakers. You can't see Vince, but you can picture him. Head starting to bob a little, a subtle wiggle in his shoulders.

All flow. No hustle.

Gary Cartwright and Bud Shrake, *Texas Monthly*

PERFECT 10

Vince Young's outstanding performance in the 2006 Rose Bowl, leading the 'Horns to the national championship, was the focus of this unique email exchange between celebrated writers Gary Cartwright and Bud Shrake as it appeared in Texas Monthly.

January 5, 2:44 PM

Bud, old amigo:

I dreamed about Vince Young last night. At least I think it was a dream. I had five or six cups of coffee watching the Rose Bowl (yeah, I know—in the old days it would have been a quart and a half of scotch), so I slept in fits and starts, like the game itself, never sure if this would end well.

But there he was, No. 10, a vision in orange striding effort-lessly across the emerald landscape, eight yards at a time, small bodies clawing at his ankles, accidental tacklers splatter-ing off his knee pads like bugs against the windshield of life, never knowing what hit them. It was one of those dreams where gravity is suspended, where everything is possible, and life is constantly renewed.

Then I woke, gathered the morning newspapers on my front lawn, and found it was true—an event so earthshaking that even the state edition of the *Dallas Morning News* had full coverage. Normally, events that happen after 9:30 at night don't reach the Austin edition for at least 36 hours. As a rule, editors at the *DMN* won't stop the presses unless, say, Houston crumbles into the Gulf of Mexico (I think they keep that story on permanent overset), but there it was on page one, in World War III type, a one-word headline that said it all: "Invincible."

Can you remember a more incredible individual perform-ance by a football player? Jim Brown against the Cowboys? Joe Namath against the Colts? John David Crow against Texas? Doak Walker against TCU? Or a more stunning moment in Longhorn history? I can't. Somehow this seems bigger than any of the three national championships that Darrell Royal won, in 1963, 1969, and 1970, when we were young and brilliant and teaching Darrell everything he knows. Or maybe I've just got a coffee hangover. I know one thing: Vince Young is the best football player I've ever seen or hope to see. And what he did in the Rose Bowl last night is something I'm going to dream about for the rest of my life.

He simply willed it to happen. When the Longhorns were down by 12 points with fewer than seven minutes to play, everyone in the country thought they were whipped—everyone but Vince, and maybe Mack Brown, whose own career was saved when he told his quarterback to stop worrying about the X's and O's and just have fun. And that's what it looked like, fun—except maybe to the bewildered USC players and fans. First, Vince methodically drove his team 69 yards in eight plays, running the final 17 himself. The extra point cut USC's lead to five, at which time the Longhorn defense made one of its infrequent appearances of the evening. Then, with 19 seconds remaining and Texas facing fourth down on the USC 8, it became clear what would happen next. Vince would take a direct snap from center, scamper out of the grasp of three or four Trojan tacklers, read a magazine, file his nails, call his momma, and head for the corner flag and his rendezvous with history. It was the easiest touchdown I ever saw.

I'm out of breath just thinking about it. I'm going to take a nap and try to forget all the ways Texas could have, and probably should have, lost this game. Wake me if I start snoring real loud.

Your pal,
Jappy [Cartwright]

January 5, 4:28 PM
Jappo:
The first time I saw Vince Young run with a football in his hands, I slapped my palms against the sides of my head the way you would to get water out of your ears, and then I rubbed my eyes and made a note to look up the word "eerie." I don't have a problem with believing we on earth have been visited by advanced life forms from other galaxies, but when you see an alien who is 6'5", weighs at least 230 pounds, wears orange and white, has huge feet, and seems to move among his fellows as if he inhabits a space no one else can enter—that is enough to send me to the dictionary. There has to be a word for it. "Eerie" does it pretty well: "suggestive of the supernatural."

There are times during a game when it looks as if everybody on the field is standing still except for Vince. He doesn't appear to be running fast (though, of course, he is) so much as everyone else is frozen in place, like in one of those party games. The proper stance in the face of mystery is awe. That's my reaction to watching him. I think, "No human could have done that." This guy is from the same planet that sent the guy to paint the ceiling of the Sistine Chapel.

Somehow I keep picturing a running back from TCU named Jim Swink. He had the same uncanny knack for running back and forth in a herd of people without anyone being able to touch him. Swink would dip and swing behind the tacklers, who suddenly found themselves running interference for him as he glided around the field. But Swink turned out not to be an alien—not a total alien, anyway, since he became a doctor—and Vince Young doesn't do that trick of circling back and dodging around. He just goes where he wants to.

No, I don't remember a more incredible individual performance by a football player. The Cowboys couldn't tackle Jim Brown, but he didn't throw passes. In the famous Super Bowl in which he had predicted his New York Jets would win against the Baltimore Colts and heavy odds, Joe Namath passed brilliantly but couldn't run at all (the Jets defense won that game, with the help of an interception by Longhorn-ex Jim Hudson). I don't remember John David Crow against Texas, though I'm sure it was memorable. I do remember Doak Walker against TCU. He had that magical bubble around him as well, and he, too, seemed to go pretty much wherever he pleased. But none of those people ever had a game like Vince Young in this Rose Bowl—or, for that matter, in last year's Rose Bowl.

Until now, James Street had my vote as the all-time best University of Texas quarterback. Street had the invincible quality about him that you mention—he never lost a game as a starter—and sparked some very dramatic events for the Longhorns. But I doubt that James would argue he could beat Vince to the goal line in a race of national champion quarterbacks who never won the Heisman Trophy.

Are you the one who thought Vince Young shouldn't start as a freshman, or was that Rush Limbaugh?

Your old amigo,
Bud

January 5, 7:45 PM

Amigo:

I don't recall the first time I saw Vince on television, but the first time I saw him with my own eyeballs was in 2004 at the Oklahoma State game, when he threw two interceptions in the first half and OSU took a four-touchdown lead. That weird sidearm motion of his looked comically inept, like a giraffe trying to shake hands with a doorknob. I turned to Ken Shine, a UT vice chancellor sitting next to me, and made the comment: "I hope that Mack Brown uses halftime to teach the boy to pass." Apparently that happened, because in the second half, Vince was perfectly on target, directing the Longhorns to six unanswered touchdowns. They won by a landslide—not that I got even a tiny bit of credit.

Does Vince still throw sidearm? I'm not sure. His passes are so effortless, mere flicks of the wrist, and so uncannily accurate that the concept of passing technique seems as obsolete as that famous coaches' caveat against scrambling quarterbacks. This guy was born to break rules, records, and hearts. He can throw on the run or falling backward or standing on his head—and still hit an ant's butt at 80 paces. And when he runs, as you say, the rest of the world seems frozen in place. He can do anything he wants on a football field, anytime he pleases, and he damn well knows it. That, my friend, is what us football guys call dangerous.

The most amazing part about last night's game is that while the Trojans had an embarrassing number of offensive weapons, Vince had to do most of the work himself. Tight end David Thomas was tough and dependable as always, but the others busted assignments, dropped balls, caused penalties, and mostly got in the way. Even the Texas defense got flustered. After the Longhorns forced USC to go three-and-out on the game's first series, Aaron Ross coughed up the ball trying to get an extra yard on a punt return. Helped along by a late hit by one of the UT linebackers, the Trojans wasted no time scoring. Then there was Mack's astonishing decision to go for it on fourth-and-one from the USC 48, with the first quarter only half done and USC up by a touchdown. Can you imagine Darrell taking such a foolish risk? Mack's blunder was compounded by offensive coordinator Greg Davis's crazy call that gave the ball to the wrong Young—Selvin instead of Vince.

But my heart truly sank after UT's first touchdown, when David Pino missed the extra point. A national championship game, and this boy misses a freaking extra point. (Later he missed a short field goal.) Teams don't blow extra points against great teams, not if they expect to win. As Abe Martin might have put it, Pino ought to buy Vince Young a cream cone.

If you remember, Darrell used to lecture on how the game had three more-or-less equal parts: offense, defense, and special teams. There was rarely a time when D.K.R. didn't have a solid kicker. Coaches don't seem concerned with that part of the game any longer. The Dallas Cowboys would be in the playoffs and might even have the home-field advantage if [Bill] Parcells and [Jerry] Jones had bothered to look for a good kicker.

I wonder if Vince can boot the old pig hide? I'll give you odds he can.

Jappy

January 5, 11:21 PM

Jappo:

You know how the TV announcers and color guys (they're called analysts now) are always making hostile remarks to each other and then acting like it's a joke and laughing heartily? They used to talk about Vince's passing motion in that same tone, like he ought to forget about throwing the ball and stick to running with it and it was silly to think otherwise. I heard one of them say there are only two reasons he completes so many passes: (1) his receivers are always open; and (2) defenses are no good. That kind of comment reminds me of the political analysis we get on the cable talk shows—it's both simple-minded and uninformed, a popular combination.

A number of critics still say that Vince will never make it as a pro because of his lack of classic form. He's a three-quarters thrower instead of a put-the-ball-up-by-your-ear-and-let-it-fly-overhand picture passer. You'd never try to teach your Pony Leaguers to throw it that way, they say. But to me, Vince's throwing motion looks very much like the one used by Drew Bledsoe, who has passed for more than 43,000 yards in the NFL, so he must be doing something right. And as you say, Vince often just flicks it. Of course, he can flick it 40 yards like a bullet. In the far-off galaxy he comes from, that's how they do it in the interplanetary games. They call it "pegging the apple."

I confess to being totally partisan about this. For the last couple of weeks, I've been wearing an orange bracelet with the Longhorn image on it that UT media legend Bill Little sent me. Stamped on the bracelet are the words "Take dead aim." The bracelets are not for sale, but they should be. I haven't read much about them in the papers, but the theme of the UT football team this season has been "Take dead aim," in honor of the 10th anniversary of Harvey Penick's death and Ben Crenshaw's downright eerie (there's that word again) winning of The Masters just a few days after Harvey's funeral.

"Take dead aim" was what Harvey called the most important message in his books. What he meant was, be aware and be in the moment. He said that once you address the ball, hitting it has got to be the most important thing in your life at that moment—that you should shut out all thoughts other than picking a target and taking dead aim, believe you're going to hit what you are aiming at, and swing away. Bill told me the coaches were looking for a theme for the 2005 season, and Mack Brown's wife, Sally, suggested "Take dead aim." I doubt if any of the players had ever heard of Harvey Penick. They weren't even born yet when Crenshaw and Tom Kite played for UT. But Mack explained to them that Harvey was a wise man and a great teacher and an Austin and a University of Texas hero—and they got it. So while you can't exactly say they dedicated this season to Harvey, he was, in spirit, a large part of it.

I did the eulogy at Harvey's funeral. Cactus Pryor sang, and Kite and Crenshaw were pallbearers. Ben cried on the plane on the way back to Augusta. People wondered if he would make it to the first tee, but there he was on Sunday, tied for the lead. I was pacing around the living room in front of my TV screen, and I felt so utterly involved that it was, well, eerie. I felt Harvey's presence there. So did Ben. If Ben hit a ball into the woods, it bounced off a tree and went back into the fairway. (If you do it from heaven, it's not cheating.) By the end of Sunday, when Ben sank the putt that won The Masters and then collapsed in tears, I was on my knees on the carpet. Ben told reporters that day that Harvey was the 15th club in his bag. The point is that a couple of those bounces at Augusta on that Sunday reminded me of certain events at the Rose Bowl—like when Vince tossed the lateral that went for a touchdown but his knee was on the ground and the replay equipment didn't get it because Harvey Penick had his thumb over the lens. And I'm sure that Harvey's spirit piled into the line on that USC fourth-down-and-two late in the fourth quarter, the play that failed because Harvey had told Reggie Bush to stay on the sidelines.

Back to the Longhorn bracelets: They ought to sell them like Lance Armstrong bracelets and split the money between the athletic department and the First Tee Harvey Penick Golf Campus.

Looking out my back windows, I can see the tower lit up orange. I can't see the big number one from here, but I just saw it on television. And we know that if we see it on television, it's real.

Bud

January 6, 10:31 AM
  Bud:
Wow! I knew the phrase "take dead aim" sounded familiar, but until now I never made the connection. Got to get one of those bracelets fast.

I found myself fighting the bitter disease of partisanship as the season wore toward what now seems like its inevitable conclusion. As sportswriters, we hated partisans ("homers," we called them). Remember that sportswriter at the *Dallas Times Herald* who always referred to the SMU Mustangs as "we," not just in conversations but in his damn columns? Pathetic. But I knew I had been infected just before Christmas when I went to the university co-op and bought my 16-year-old grandson, Malcolm, an orange UT coach's jacket and a white No. 10 Longhorn jersey. Malcolm lives in Little Rock, Arkansas, but I'm hoping he gets the fever. Just to be sure, I'm going out today to buy him a poster of the orange tower with the big number one on its face.

In retrospect, the Longhorns didn't just have Harvey's eternal spirit in their locker room, they had the living legend of Darrell Royal, too. Darrell and his wife, Edith, were ubiquitous in Pasadena—Darrell his usual strong, quiet, laid-back presence, and Edith making sure nobody missed the symbolism. There was a funny moment at the front gate of the Rose Bowl when security stopped Darrell and Edith because he wasn't wearing his credentials. "Delbert" (remember when we nicknamed him Delbert?) didn't bother mentioning that he had coached three national championship teams at UT. But when they tried to force him through a metal detector, Edith took charge. "He's got a pacemaker," she scolded. "He's not going anywhere."

As I recall, we coined the name Delbert after UT's first national championship season, in 1963. He had just been named Coach of the Year and was hiding out from the press. So naturally he came to Dallas and concealed himself in an apartment on Cole Avenue occupied by two sportswriters named Shrake and Cartwright. Perfect plan, heh? "Delbert" was so that nobody would know his true identity. Four decades later, I still call him that. By the way, do you and Delbert play golf semiregularly anymore, or has age rained you out?

Inevitably, people will compare Mack and Darrell. There are similarities, not the least of which is that they both won national championships. Both are solid, fundamental, and charismatic. Like Darrell, Mack knows exactly who he is and what he's about. Mack has been criticized for being too conservative, too uptight, and too nice. Forty years ago you could have said the same about Darrell, though nobody did. They're from different generations. The game has changed.

Darrell's offense was once ridiculed as three-yards-and-a-cloud-of-dust, even though his 1969 national champions were the highest-scoring offense in UT history until this year. Vince Young throws more passes in a game than Darrell's teams threw in a season. Darrell's creed was that two out of the three things that can happen when you throw a pass are bad, but he knew when and where to use the weapon. Remember the 1964 Cotton Bowl, number one UT against number two Navy and its Heisman Trophy quarterback, Roger Staubach? The best passer that day wasn't Staubach but UT's Duke Carlisle. The game is still about blocking and tackling. Darrell knew that, and so does Mack.

Before the Rose Bowl, a lot of people were calling USC the greatest team in college history. Now they're wondering if this UT team is better than the UT team of 1969. It's a question without an answer. Vince Young would have made one hell of a wishbone quarterback, though I'm not altogether certain he would have beat out James Street.

Jappy

January 6, 12:59 PM

Jappo:

I seem to remember that the Friday night before the Texas-Oklahoma game in 1963, when Darrell phoned the Cole Avenue apartment, you answered and asked him what brings him to town. That's about as unpartisan as it gets. I get a kick out of the image of you buying an orange coach's jacket and a white jersey for your grandson all these years later. You have gained in wisdom as you have matured, little grasshopper.

I feel sorry for people who can't get a thrill out of a major event like this year's Rose Bowl game and the national championship coming back to Austin after a 35-year absence. I'm not just talking about Aggies: I mean people who don't get emotionally involved in sports. They are missing something important in life. Everybody should have a team—actually, several teams—to root for. The greatest thing about it is that there's always next season. No matter how good or how bad this season was, we'll get 'em next year. Unless you're a fan of the Texas Rangers baseball team, in which case we may not get 'em, since we never have. But as a sports fan, there is nearly always something new going on, another game coming up, another chance for redemption. And you change sports as the seasons change. Love affairs bloom and fade, and new love affairs begin. So partisanship in sports is something to take pleasure in.

I should admit that I don't actually go to very many sporting events these days (and I didn't go to the Rose Bowl). That's why television was invented. For 25 years, when I was writing for *Sports Illustrated* and various newspapers, I was paid to go to sporting events, and I always had a parking pass. Two things stop me from going these days: parking and instant replay. Mostly I just go to Lady Longhorns basketball games. I'm a big fan of the team, and I'm suffering with this freshman group as they grow up. And I went to the Roller Derby last summer at the Thunderdome. (By the way, that A&E reality series on Austin's Lonestar Rollergirls is a winner.) But not going to the games doesn't mean I don't care. I'm a TCU grad, and they went 11–1. I spent my sophomore year at the University of Texas, and I live in Austin, and I am 13–0 with the Longhorns. My 24–1 season is something to be unashamedly partisan about.

Yes, Jap, I remember when we started calling Darrell "Delbert." We went to some social gathering and he didn't want people to know who he was, so we introduced him as Delbert. And it worked. A few weeks later, after the national championship, he was about as anonymous as the Beatles. That's what I mean about sports. As one of baseball's wise men, Yogi Berra, probably said, "Your future is always ahead of you."

Bud

January 8, 6:09 PM

Bud:

If you've been watching TV, you know already that Vince Young ruined my Sunday and possibly the remainder of 2006 and the start of 2007. The ingrate just announced he's turning pro. A pox on his house.

Okay, maybe I'm overreacting. I admit that his draft stock in the NFL will never be higher. Vince said that he made the decision after talking to his momma and his pastor. He promised them that he'd come back and finish his degree. Presumably they reminded him that he's certain to be one of the top three choices, which means he'll be guaranteed about $25 million. We all need sound adult advice from time to time.

If the Houston Texans, who have the first choice in the draft, don't grab homeboy Vince, they're even dumber than I think they are. I hear that they're still set on Reggie Bush. The only way Bush can help that miserable franchise is if they can trade him for five Pro Bowl linemen.

Looking at it realistically, what else could Vince prove at Texas? Sure, he could return for his senior year, maybe win the Heisman, help UT extend its winning streak to 33, and possibly even win a second-straight title game. Or he could blow out his knee against Sam Houston State.

Vince's afternoon press conference came as a shock to nearly everyone. Six or seven hours earlier, I'd awakened from my nightly Vince dream, already sweating next season, calculating like some miser scouring his coin purse how the Longhorns can possibly replace AP All-Americans like offensive tackle Jonathan Scott and defensive tackle Rod Wright, not to mention half of the best secondary in college football. Then I remembered that Michael Griffin—whose amazing interception at the corner of the goal line was to me the defensive play of the game—will return, as will some fantastic skill players, such as Jamaal Charles, Ramonce Taylor, Billy Pittman, Quan Cosby, and Limas Sweed. No coach in America has a better supply of talent waiting in the wings than Mack Brown, and having his face on Wheaties boxes can't hurt.

What Mack doesn't have—I mean, who does?—is another Vince Young. The Longhorns will go into next season with a quarterback who has never played a down of college football. Forget another national championship. Mack will be lucky to make it to the Sun Bowl.

Let us pause now and be thankful for what we had. Let us hope it will come again. Let us forget that it won't.

Jap

January 8, 6:56 PM

Jappo:

So he's gone to the great NFL in the sky. The realist in me says he would never have had another peak experience in college to match the one he had at the Rose Bowl. That beautiful photo in the *Austin American-Statesman* of him standing in the midst of a shower of colored bits of something (was that confetti or the air in Los Angeles?) said it all. If he had come back to UT for his senior season, even as loaded with talent as the Longhorns are, it's a long, dangerous road to next year's championship. So he would have had to come back for his teammates and not just for himself.

And, of course, there was the elephant in the room. It is called "medial collateral ligament." Tear one of those, and no physical genius is ever the same again. Out the window would go tens of millions of dollars, not only for playing professional football, but for endorsements. Vince is a total natural for endorsements. He's got the smile and the ease, and he looks good on television. Now he can start cashing in on his personality. There are many things in life more important than money, especially if you've already got some of it in the bank. Now he's protected from a financial disaster that would have come with injury. Of course, Vince will never get injured. In the galaxy he comes from, they may have bred bodies that won't break. Just think of the preseason publicity that would have been lavished on Texas if he had come back. It would make Elvis Presley's manager blush.

Having decided to take the money and run, may he be guided into the right professional organization by the wizards of his galaxy. The summer after O. J. Simpson won the Heisman Trophy at USC, in 1968, I went with him to the Buffalo Bills training camp. Remember how Puss Erwin at the *Fort Worth Press* used to punch you in the chest with his knobby finger and say, "You'll never make it, son"? The Buffalo coach took a look at O.J. and said he would never make it in the NFL as a running back. So O.J. wasted his first few seasons on special teams before a new coach turned him loose to break records as a running back. Surely such a thing will never happen to Vince Young.

The bright side is now we can watch him play 20 times a year.

Happy days,
Bud

Head coach Darrell Royal (left) was a gracious winner with Oklahoma's Chuck Fairbanks in 1967, despite a pregame controversy that almost eclipsed the Longhorns' 9–7 win.

Section III
THE COACHES

David Condon, *Chicago Tribune*

TEXAS-IRISH BOWL TILT RECALLS DAYS OF CHEVIGNY

On the occasion of the Texas–Notre Dame clash in the Cotton Bowl of 1970, Chicago Tribune *writer David Condon recalled Jack Chevigny, the man who coached Texas to a major upset of Notre Dame in 1934, six years after he starred in Notre Dame's famous "Win one for the Gipper" victory over Army and who later died heroically as a first lieutenant at the battle of Iwo Jima in World War II.*

The former University of Texas football coach died the way you'd expect a Hoosier and Texan to die. Jack Chevigny, always a fighter, died as he lived: he died in his customary role of leading the attack.

Death came to Jack Chevigny, one of the famous football men of his time, as one of the first waves of Americans to hit Iwo Jima on the first day of the invasion. Chevigny was a marine lieutenant.

Today, with thousands of fans awaiting the Cotton Bowl football game between Texas and Notre Dame, memories of Jack Chevigny are kindled anew. He knew gridiron glory both at Notre Dame and at Texas. How Jack became a part of Notre Dame's most storied football legend will be revealed as this morning's essay unwinds.

Chevigny was a high school star in Hammond, Indiana, when national headlines were being made by Knute Rockne and his Four Horsemen, the only other Notre Dame team ever to accept a bowl game invitation. Chev matriculated at Notre Dame, only a punt and a pass from Hammond.

Chevigny was a senior halfback on Notre Dame's 1928 11. This was the team that Rockne labeled the Minute Men because "they are in the game only a minute before the other team scores." This was the weakest team Rockne ever had at Notre Dame, and [it] lost four games. The 1928 squad just didn't have enough men like Jack Chevigny.

Rock called Chev "the best right halfback in Notre Dame history." He was one of the greatest of Irish blockers ever. He was a defensive ace.

After Jack Chevigny was graduated, he stayed at Notre Dame as Rock's assistant and was a brilliant backfield coach for the 1929 and 1930 national champions. The backs he coached were legendary—Frank Carideo, Joe Savoldi, Jack Elder, Marty Brill, Marchy Schwartz, and Moon Mullins.

Early in 1931, Chevigny agreed to leave Notre Dame for a top assistant's post on the West Coast. Tragedy changed his mind. Rockne died in a plane crash on March 31, 1931, and a few days later, Reverend Charles L. O'Donnell announced: "There is no head coach at Notre Dame. Knute Rockne is always the head coach. Hunk Anderson will be the senior coach, and Jack Chevigny the junior coach."

Chevigny served one year as aide to Anderson. Then the pro Chicago Cardinals were seeking a replacement for Ernie Nevers, the All-Everything from Stanford. Dr. David Jones, owner of the Cardinals, grabbed Chevigny to coach in 1932.

The next year, a little Texas college—St. Edward's—operated by the same order that runs Notre Dame, wanted a head coach. They offered Chevigny $4,200 a year. The Cardinals' Dr. Jones said: "A pro team that plays only three months a year cannot meet that price." Chev went to St. Edward's with the best wishes of all.

He had such a successful season that the University of Texas hired him to replace Clyde Littlefield.

Chevigny brought the Texas Longhorns back to Notre Dame in 1934. It was his first game as Texas coach. It was also the Notre Dame coaching debut of Elmer Layden, the Four Horsemen fullback. The odds were against Texas; Notre Dame hadn't lost an opener in 38 years!

But Notre Dame's George Melinkovich (remember) fumbled the opening kick-off. Texas recovered on the Irish 17. Instants later, John Hilliard crashed 8 yards for a touchdown and kicked the point, giving Texas a 7–0 lead.

In the second quarter, Buster Baebel of Texas fumbled Andy Pilney's punt when hit by John Michuta. Michuta recovered for Notre Dame on the Texas 9. On fourth down, Melinkovich smashed one yard for an Irish touchdown. Wayne Millner missed the kick for the point. Texas led, 7–6.

That's the way it ended, too. Jack Chevigny had coached Texas to victory—its only conquest of Notre Dame in history.

Chevigny stayed at Texas for three seasons, compiling a 14–14–2 record. He yielded the coaching reins to Nebraska's Dana X. Bible, the greatest of all Longhorn football chieftains.

Time went on. Chevigny was around and about. When war came along, he wanted to be a part of it. He joined the marines. A power in

Washington offered him an armchair job. Chevigny snorted: "Marines are expendable."

Inevitably, the end came on bloody Iwo.

It was then that old friends, mourning the Notre Dame and Texas football man, began remembering the Army game of 1928. That was the Gipper's day.

Army, led by Chris Cagle, was an unbeaten powerhouse when it took the field against Notre Dame's Minute Men in Yankee Stadium. Notre Dame was as green as St. Patrick's Day in Dublin.

So as the Fighting Irish headed for certain defeat, Rockne told 'em a story. Eight years before he had been standing at George Gipp's deathbed, and Gipp had said: "Someday, Rock, when things are going against the boys, and they aren't getting the breaks, tell 'em to go out and win one for the Gipper. I don't know where I'll be, but I'll know, and I'll be happy."

Winding up his tale of the Gipper, Rock said softly: "Men, this is that day."

The first half was scoreless as mighty Army outplayed the weary but determined Irish. The game still was scoreless when Chevigny finally crashed across the cadet goal line. Here Jack Chevigny continued into the end zone, pitched the football high in the air, and gave the now famous cry: "There's one for the Gipper."

Army tied the score at 6–6. But the Irish were aroused by Chevigny's battle cry. There was a fumble, though, and Army men charged for the loose ball. From nowhere, Jack Chevigny appeared to pounce on it. Then the Irish heard Chevigny mumbling incoherently, apparently injured from a prior play.

Rock sent in another halfback, Johnny Niemiec. He also sent in an end, Johnny O'Brien, thereafter renowned as One-Play O'Brien.

In that era, substitutes couldn't talk to the team until one play had elapsed. Carideo, the Notre Dame quarterback, sensed the play Rock wanted. It was fourth and 16.

The ball went to Niemiec. Johnny passed 40 yards to One-Play O'Brien, who stumbled across for the winning touchdown. Final score: Notre Dame 12, Army 6.

That was Jack Chevigny's greatest Notre Dame day. His greatest at Texas was beating Notre Dame. Thanks for the memories, Jack.

W. K. Stratton, *Backyard Brawl*

BIBLE AND GOD

In this excerpt from Backyard Brawl, *his book about the Texas–Texas A&M rivalry, W. K. Stratton addresses the contributions made by Texas coach Dana X. Bible.*

It always seemed curious to me that the improbably named Dana Xenophon Bible hasn't been more exalted in Texas than he has been. I asked sportswriter and novelist Dan Jenkins about that once, and he said that Bible came off a little bit on the stuffy side. I'm guessing he didn't talk much about buzzard puke.

Stuffiness aside, Bible was a great coach and, remarkably enough, had a course-changing impact on both the A&M and UT programs. And Nebraska's, too, for what it's worth. Born in Jefferson County, Tennessee, in 1891, he was a three-sport athlete at Carson-Newman College and the University of North Carolina before he became the football coach at Mississippi College. After brief stints as freshman coach at A&M and temporary head coach at LSU, he returned to A&M as head football coach and athletic director in 1917—he was all of 26 years old.

Youth aside, he was a coaching fool. His first Aggie squad won all eight of its games and claimed the school's first Southwest Conference title. He took 1918 off to help America and the Allies win what was then optimistically called the War to End All Wars, during which he piloted one of those newfangled flying machines. Then he came back to A&M in 1919 to lead the Aggies to a 10–0 record and another Southwest Conference title. He had another undefeated team in 1927. He compiled a record of 72–19–9, with six Southwest Conference championships, before he departed to coach the Cornhuskers following the 1928 season.

His coaching style was [patterned after] Knute Rockne's: build up your players, make them think they could achieve the impossible. He didn't have a Gipper, but in November 1922, playing the Longhorns in Austin, with the score tied 7–7 at the half, he dragged his foot across the visitors' locker room and said, "Men, those who want to go out and be known as members of an A&M team that defeated Texas in Austin, step over the line." With their record at 4–4, the outcome of the Texas game would determine if they had a winning season. The Fightin' Farmers tripped all over themselves to step over the line, then went out and scored seven more points while holding Texas scoreless. A&M went back to College Station with a 14–7 victory and a 5–4 season.

Nothing Bible did at A&M was nearly as significant as a decision he made in January 1922, when he started the tradition of the 12th Man. The Aggies were in Dallas for their first-ever bowl game, the Dixie Classic (a precursor to the Cotton Bowl). They faced Centre College of Danville, Kentucky, a Presbyterian college that had upended the flapper-era football world that fall by defeating Harvard, mighty Harvard, which had not lost a game in five years and was the number-one team in the country. The defeat of the Crimson by the Praying Colonels often is cited as the biggest sports upset of the 20th century. The Fightin' Presbyterians and the Fightin' Farmers played a tough game that day. So much so that Aggie E. King Gill received a summons that was totally unexpected. King Gill recalled what happened:

> I had played on the football team but was on the basketball team at that time, and those in charge felt I was more valuable to the basketball team. I was in Dallas, however, and even rode to the stadium in the same taxi with Coach Bible. I was in civilian clothes and was not to be in uniform. Coach Bible asked me to assist in spotting players for the late Jinx Tucker [sports editor of the *Waco News-Tribune*] in the press box. So I was up in the press box helping Jinx when, near the end of the first half, I was called down to the Texas A&M bench. There had been a number of injuries, but it was not until I arrived on the field that I learned that Coach Bible wanted me to put on a football uniform and play if he needed me. There were no dressing rooms at the stadium in those days. The team had dressed downtown at the hotel and traveled to the stadium in taxicabs. Anyway, I put on the uniform of one of the injured players. We got under the stands, and he [the player] put on my clothes and I put on his uniform. I was ready to play but never was sent into the game.

A&M downed Centre 22–14.

As far as tradition and the spirit of Aggieland and a few steel guitar idylls are concerned, it's a good thing Dr. Gill swapped clothes with the injured player underneath the stands and was ready but not actually called onto the field. The *e pluribus unum* of the Aggies has been known ever since as the 12th Man. All Aggies are ready to go out onto whatever metaphoric playing field to which they are beckoned when the need arises. That's why the entire student section, not to mention a good number of the former students, stands throughout each game. Outside Kyle Field, there's a statue of Dr. Gill in his football uniform, ready to go. It gleams in the sunshine just like the statue of Sully [Lawrence Sullivan Ross] up the way.

With a good won-loss record at A&M, the Aggies' first bowl appearance, and the 12th Man legend to his credit, Bible notched out a place on the roll of Texas coaching greats. But he wasn't finished.

He left A&M and made Nebraska a football powerhouse. He was 50–15–7 in eight seasons at Nebraska and claimed half a dozen Big 6 championships. But the fact is that you can't find a proper chicken-fried steak, bowl of chili, or barbecued brisket in the whole of Nebraska. Or something was missing for him in Nebraska. The story goes that he wanted to return to Texas. And the University of Texas was anxious to have him.

Just before midnight on November 29, 1893, an alleged football team of fewer than 20 players boarded a train in Austin for a trip to Fairgrounds Park in Dallas. About a hundred fans accompanied these upstarts on the train, according to Lou Maysel in his thorough accounting of the history of UT football through 1970, *Here Come the Longhorns*. This was so long ago that burnt orange hadn't been invented yet. The fans wore what were then the UT school colors: gold and white. The next day, Thanksgiving Day, the fans in Dallas engaged in an actual yell practice—imagine that, teasips (that all-purpose pejorative Aggies have for Longhorns) practicing yells. Maysel reports their favorite yell was:

Hullabaloo, hullabaloo,
'Ray, 'ray, 'ray.
Hoo-ray, hoo-ray,
Varsity, varsity, UTA

At Fairgrounds Park, the UT team went up against the Dallas Foot Ball Club, which had not lost a game since about the time the last of the Comanches were exiled to Oklahoma. The sports prognosticators of the day predicted a blowout for the Dallas club, and of course Texas won, 18–16. A lot of guys who bet against the line went out on a spree of sarsaparilla drinking that night, snapping their shirt garters at every woman they met and leaving large tips for every barbershop quartet they heard. And the University of Texas football tradition was born. UT finished the season 4–0, 'ray, 'ray, 'ray.

For the next 40 years, Texas was consistently good (you have to look all the way up to 1933 before you find the first losing season), although there seemed to be a steady churn around the program as coaches came and went. But by 1936, the Longhorns were bottom-dwellers in the Southwest Conference. To bring stability to the program, Texas looked to Lincoln, Nebraska, and made Bible an earth-shaking offer: a 20-year contract, the first 10 as head coach and athletic director, the last 10 solely as athletic director. For this, he would receive a starting salary of $15,000—double what UT president H. Y. Benedict made, triple what the highest-paid university professor made. And at a time when most people in America walked around with holes in their shoes, singing "Buddy, Can You Spare a Dime?" Bible had been making $12,000 at Nebraska. By comparison, his Texas predecessor, Jack Chevigny, made only $5,000. But Bible always maintained the salary wasn't what brought him to Texas. No, no—it wasn't *that* much different from what he made heading the Cornhuskers' program. It was the opportunity, the challenge.

The Longhorns were terrible his first two seasons, but off the field, Bible had things working. He had divided the state into districts and put members of the Ex-Students' Association in charge of recruiting the best players in their districts for Texas.

The so-called Bible Plan was thus born.

By 1940, thanks to the recruits the plan brought in, the 'Horns were back. If you needed proof, you could have just looked at the Thanksgiving matchup with Bible's old team, the Aggies. A&M was at its peak as a football power. The year before, it had claimed its first and only national championship. The Aggies were the favorites to be invited to the Rose Bowl to take on the best of the West Coast, Stanford. All they had to do was beat Texas in Austin and wrap up the Southwest Conference title. It seemed they should be able to do just that. They'd humiliated the Longhorns in College Station the year before, 20–0, on their way to their national crown. But Texas managed to score on four plays in the first 58 seconds of the game, including the "impossible catch" by Noble Doss, then protected the 7–0 lead for the next 59 minutes and two seconds. Goodbye, Pasadena. Hello, Dallas and the Cotton Bowl for the Aggies. A&M coach Homer Norton told his team, "This is perhaps the bitterest pill you will ever have to swallow, but there's one good thing about it. If you can take what happened to you today as a lesson for when you go out into life, and don't get cocky and overconfident at some other time, then this defeat might not be as bad as it seems." After saying this, Dan Jenkins wrote in *I'll Tell You One Thing,* Norton found solitude in a corner and wept. As Norton cried, the Longhorns were dancing with joy.

Between 1940 and when Bible stepped down from the head coach's job, Texas was 53–13–3, with three Southwest Conference titles and three appearances in the Cotton Bowl. His overall coaching record ended up at 192–71–23, a .712 winning percentage, which was good enough to get him inducted into the College Football Hall of Fame and to get his name on several lists of the 50 best college football coaches of all time.

But his big contribution was bringing stability to a program grown rickety. That and he hired Darrell K. Royal.

Terry Frei, *Horns, Hogs, and Nixon Coming*

COACH ROYAL

Terri Frei took an in-depth look at Darrell Royal from the years between his 1963 and 1969 National Championship teams in this chapter from Horns, Hogs, and Nixon Coming, *his provocative and enlightening account of the 1969 Texas-Arkansas game and the events surrounding the contest.*

A national championship brought you only so much time at the University of Texas, and by the spring of 1968 Darrell Royal was five years removed from coaching the Longhorns to an undefeated season and the number-one ranking. That 1963 defense, led by sophomore linebacker Tommy Nobis and senior defensive lineman Scott Appleton, was dominating. The Longhorns lost their best offensive threat, halfback Ernie Koy, to a shoulder separation at midseason and still went undefeated and beat Roger Staubach and the Navy Midshipmen in the Cotton Bowl. The national championship came in Royal's seventh season in Austin, when he was only 39.

Yet that raised the standards even higher. More than ever, winning at Texas didn't mean winning seasons, it meant dominating the Southwest Conference and lording it over every one of the six other Texas-based schools in the league. It meant providing the best punch-lines of all for Texas Aggie jokes (e.g., "27–0"). It meant going to the Cotton Bowl every January 1 and landing virtually every high school prospect the Longhorns sought in the state, whether the prospect was going to play or ultimately just be kept away from Texas Tech or Southern Methodist or even Rice. And it meant beating the Big 8 Conference's Oklahoma Sooners every year in the heated Red River rivalry in Dallas, enabling the UT boosters to continue forgiving Royal for being an "Okie."

The Longhorns' coach had been forced to grow up fast in Hollis, Oklahoma. His mother, Katy, died in October 1924, when Darrell—her sixth child—was only three months old. When he was 16, his father moved the family to California. Darrell hated the West Coast and got permission from his dad, Burley Ray, to return to Oklahoma on his own. After his high school graduation in Hollis, Darrell had an offer to play football at Oklahoma, but he went into the Army Air Corps in 1943 and eventually was trained as a tail gunner on a B-24 bomber. His crew was held back from being sent overseas to be trained for photo reconnaissance missions, and he still was in the United States when the war ended. In the fall of 1945, he played for the Third Air Force football team, based in Tampa, and was heavily re-recruited by the college coaches. He was a prized prospect, although he weighed only 158 pounds, and he went to OU to play for Jim Tatum. As a senior All-American quarterback in 1949, Royal was 25 years old and playing under Tatum's young successor, Bud Wilkinson. To the press, Wilkinson touted his quarterback as a heady coaching candidate, and writers willingly ran with the suggestion, as when Walter Stewart of the *Memphis Commercial-Appeal* wrote after the 1950 Sugar Bowl that Royal "owns one of the most brilliant masses of football cerebellum we've seen caged in one skull. ... [T]hat night, he gave us a clinical critique which was magnificently lucid and economically complete. He'll make someone a game-winning coach."

Royal's first college job was as an assistant at North Carolina State in 1950. In 1973's *The Darrell Royal Story*, author Jimmy Banks wrote that even before Royal was on the sideline for his first game, he considered quitting the business because he discovered he was petrified of public speaking, which was part of the job for even assistant coaches. As dynamic as he could be in informal situations or with small groups, standing on a podium was torture for him at first. But he managed to keep his poise and get through a lecture about his experiences as a split-T quarterback, and about the offense itself, at a coaching clinic on the University of Tennessee campus that July, and the big-name coaches in attendance—familiar with him as a quarterback—found they agreed with the Memphis columnist's assessment. Royal was stamped as a hot coaching prospect before he had coached in a game, and his knowledge of the hot offense of the period—the split T—was coveted.

After that season, Tulsa coach Buddy Brothers offered Royal a raise and a promotion to a number-one assistant's job, and Royal verbally accepted it. Before he signed a contract, though, Bud Wilkinson called and offered him a job on the OU staff. Royal wanted to take it, but when Brothers made it clear he believed Royal would be going back on his word, the young coach swallowed hard and went to Tulsa. As it turned out, Royal loved the experience because Brothers allowed him—a college QB only two seasons earlier—complete freedom to run the offense, and the Hurricanes lost only once. Royal's bona fides as a precocious coach were solidified, and Mississippi State coach Murray Warmath hired him away.

Then Royal took the unusual step of accepting the head job with the Edmonton Eskimos of the Canadian Football League's forerunner, the Western Interprovincial Football Union—for a garish $13,500.

North of the border, football was a game of limited resources, 12 players, legal forward motion at the snap, a 55-yard line, and a "rouge" single point when the opposition couldn't get the ball out of the end zone. It also was Royal's chance to get his legs as a head coach, and the Eskimos were 1–7–5. Royal cited the experience when he talked with Mississippi State about returning—this time as the head coach. He went 12–8 in two seasons in Starkville, then 5–5 in a salmon-out-of-water season at the University of Washington in 1956. When the Texas job opened up, Royal left Washington with three years remaining on his contract and became the Longhorns' head coach in 1957—a year ahead of Frank Broyles's move to Arkansas. Royal was 17–13 as a college head coach when he went to Texas, but he was only eight seasons removed from being an All-American quarterback and had only solidified his image as an offensive genius.

One of the naïve assumptions in sports, whether expressed in the media or in the casual chatter of fans, is that players on any team have a monolithic, easily summarized opinion of their coach. Particularly in the late 1960s, it was difficult to be a beloved and winning college football head coach at the same time. Some of the best molders of young men and best-loved coaches *weren't* aloof and did heavily invest their emotions in their players. But that could eat them up, and when they were fired or they resigned, it could be said: *just not tough enough to be a great head coach.*

Above all, it was—and is—perilous to overgeneralize, even about Frank Broyles. That said, summarizing the players' views of the Arkansas coach for the most part painted a fair picture. With Royal at Texas, it was far more complex. The Longhorns felt a mixture of fear, respect, hatred, anger, confusion, and reverence—and all of those emotions could swirl within one player. Over the years, those who stuck it out in the Royal program tended to forget the rest and remember the respect, and add to it. It's a fair exchange: If they stuck with Royal, he stuck with them, moving mountains for his former players over the years.

"If he never said your name the entire time, you'd be very happy," 1969 guard Mike Dean says of him. "You were scared to death of him, literally scared to death of him. I don't know anybody who wasn't scared to death. Afterward, I realized what he was doing. He told me one time that he practiced a system he called intermittent reinforcement. You never knew if he liked you or he didn't like you. He told me, 'If I was down on you all the time, you'd quit the team. If all I did was praise you, you'd let up.' You never knew where you stood with him. One day he would praise you and the next day he'd make you feel like a piece of dirt. Because of this, we all feared him. To be honest, we didn't really like him. We certainly respected him. I love the man now, but at the time, I just knew if he said my name, it wasn't going to be good."

Linebacker Scott Henderson, a junior in 1969, says of Royal, "Some people thought he was ruthless. Some people thought he was unfair. I always found him to be fair—tough, but fair."

Tight end Randy Peschel says Royal "was a psychologist and motivator second to none. He knew what buttons to push to get you to do what you needed to. I know my appreciation grew for him exponentially after I was done. Maybe others did, but I know I didn't realize at the time what he was doing and how he was doing it and how he was helping me and all of us as a team."

Royal, meanwhile, earned his players' complicated opinion of him by overseeing a sometimes brutal regimen: The "shit" treatment for the scrubs in the Texas program, involving extra practice work, wasn't unique in college football in the 1960s, and it generated bitterness in those who felt they were being punished—or run off. The Monday "Turd Bowls," matching those who hadn't played on Saturday against the freshmen, were legendary for both their sharp-edged competitiveness and their implicit punishment. The upperclassmen were angry at having to play on Mondays and not Saturdays. "It was the freshmen against everybody in the world," says 1969 All-American tackle Bob McKay, who went through the Turd Bowls as a freshman in 1966. "The sophomores were the worst because they had just gotten out of it, and they treated you like shit anyway. They just took delight in trying to kick your ass, so you had to learn pretty quick that you had to stand up for yourself, and the only friends you had were the other freshmen."

Similarly infamous were the off-season conditioning drills under veteran trainer Frank Medina—drills that some players concluded were tougher for the marginal players. "Medina was somewhat of a henchman," guard Bobby Mitchell says. "He was running people off, really." Others thought Medina's workout program was egalitarian hell. "He was the one who kept us in shape," Mike Dean says. "We were in incredible shape, and he deserves some credit for our success." Regardless, Medina considered the workouts biblical trials, challenging the Longhorns to measure their faith. It also was rationalized as a Darwinian test in a tough sport: Only the strong would survive, and maybe they even would contribute to the program. If they stuck it out but didn't play, they still would be stronger and better men for it, wouldn't they? And if they didn't survive, if they quit or dropped out of the program, they weren't strong enough to be missed.

That's just how it was.

The numbers game was cold: Texas annually brought in about 50 scholarship freshman players, the elite of the state's prospects. Even when the lack of a ceiling on the total number of scholarship players in the program lessened the need for attrition, the numbers were unmanageable if all the scholarship players remained in the program. If they left cussing your program, that wasn't a tragedy. They hadn't been playing for anyone else in the league. If they transferred, it often was to where they could play right away, and that wasn't possible within the Southwest Conference because of the transfer rules. It's naïve to assume that everyone who left did so *only* or even primarily because of the physical rigors; players didn't like seeing their name on a little circular disk hanging in the seventh slot below the position name on the depth chart board, and they often wanted to go somewhere they could play. Or they decided to end their college football careers on the spot. But if they stayed with Royal and the Longhorns, they knew they were subject to exhausting physical workouts and caustic reviews.

"When Coach Royal came off his tower at practice, you hoped to hell he turned right because that meant the defense screwed up and it wasn't us," McKay says. "The thing is, it was a different time. We didn't ask questions. When we were told to do something...hell, there were 300 people on the field at any one time. If you didn't like the way things were going, they didn't give a shit, you were more than welcome to leave. It wasn't, 'Well, do we think this is going to work, do we really want to do this?' It wasn't up for discussion."

As the head of that Texas program, Royal *was* universally respected, if the definition included the understanding that he was the supreme power. When the Longhorns gathered on Sunday to watch game film as a full team, there was plenty of collegial chatter in the room as players filed in, sat down, and waited. Then, as Royal walked in from the back, the silence followed him up the aisle like a wave, until those in the first few rows sensed it and shut up even before the coach passed them.

And the odds were pretty strong that none of the players in the room would have a personal conversation with Royal any time soon. In Fayetteville, Arkansas, Frank Broyles seemed uncomfortable with closeness; in Austin, Texas, Darrell Royal seemed disdainful of it. Everyone understood that, including Bob McKay and defensive tackle Leo Brooks, both stars. "A guy from a newspaper out in West Texas, where we were from, talked to us, and he couldn't understand that we just didn't walk in and talk with Coach Royal," McKay says. "That would be like me going to play with rattlesnakes. I'm smart enough to know that you don't do that. Coach Royal was always nice, but he was Coach Royal. I didn't stop in to shoot the shit. It wasn't something you did for fun. I told that kid I was in his office five times in my college career, and four of them weren't worth a damn." The fifth, McKay said, was late in the 1969 season when Royal called him in and told him he had been named an All-American, but that he needed to keep it quiet until the official announcement. At the Thanksgiving game at Texas A&M, Royal saw McKay's parents after the game and congratulated them. They asked why.

Later, Royal approached McKay.

"You didn't tell 'em?"

"No, sir, you told me not to tell anybody, so I didn't tell anybody."

Royal's authority was unquestioned. Yet by Texas standards, Royal's program struggled mightily from 1965 to 1967. At Texas, 6–4 records were abominable, and that was their record in each of the three regular seasons. The Longhorns beat Mississippi after the 1966 season in the Bluebonnet Bowl to finish 7–4, but Royal vetoed any thought of going to a bowl game after the 1967 season. The Longhorns didn't deserve to go anywhere, he declared. It really didn't matter all that much that the Texas boosters—the men with the money and the influence—were applying heat because Royal was plenty hot himself. He was going to do something about it, ordering that the 1968 spring training and the 1968 fall practices be living hell. He didn't even try to pretend it was something other than a test. The candy asses, those who couldn't take it, those who didn't want it bad enough, were going to be gone, one way or another.

"We were coming off three 6–4s," Royal says of the 1968 practices. "You bet it was hard. You always do that. You always had it stern enough to find out who wanted to and who didn't. Who wanted to late? Who wanted to when you were behind? Who wanted to when they were tired? Who wanted to when it would be easier to take a lazy step or two? You have to push them hard enough to find that out."

By 1968 Royal was ahead of his time in one area, disdaining water deprivation, which was a part of the testing mechanism for so long, from coast to coast: In 1962 reserve sophomore guard Reggie Grob suffered heatstroke during fall practice, went into a coma, and died four days before the season opener in Austin against the University of Oregon Ducks. Royal's angst was palpable, and he openly talked and agonized about whether he and his staff should have been able to prevent Grob's death.

"Coach Royal had gone through a tough time when that kid had died," guard Randy Stout says. "We always had water—all the time."

In 1968 they weren't thirsty, but they were so sore they often couldn't even make the walk from the stadium to the football dorm, or vice versa, on the way to the second practice of the day in the fall, without stopping or lying down to rest. Royal's pride and his job were on the line, and if he was going to go down, he was going to go down with the toughest.

"I wasn't surprised that it was that tough," Scott Henderson says of 1968 spring ball. "I *was* surprised that so many guys quit and left. But Royal made it very clear it was going to be whoever wants to play."

Henderson had undergone knee surgery after his freshman season, so he was watching the practices, not participating. The rehabilitation from his surgery to repair a torn anterior cruciate ligament was difficult, but Henderson wasn't sure it was any worse than what he witnessed on the field.

Bob McKay was more certain. He had to drop out of spring ball to have rotator cuff surgery. "I swore to God, I was the happiest man in the world when I got to go to the hospital."

Bill Zapalac, then a sophomore-to-be tight-end who turned into a star linebacker for the 1969 team, says those spring drills were "hellacious, and they weeded out some of the upperclassmen. I don't know if it was intentional, but a lot of people quit."

The survivors added it up: about 30 players quit, and about 30 more were hurt in spring ball. They weren't just the scrubs, either. Tommy Orr was expected to challenge to start at tackle. *Gone.* Jack Freeman, the guy in the dorm room next to McKay, had played for Odessa's Permian High School, where they were as tough as they come. *Gone.* McKay managed to say good-bye, but star tight end Deryl Comer—McKay's roommate—was so drained he couldn't even get up. Freeman understood. Comer himself "quit" during spring drills, but came back after a day. Everyone understood that the staff wouldn't have let him come back—he paid for his impudence with extra sprints—if he had been a Turd Bowl regular.

Survivors, such as undersized and unheralded guard Mike Dean, saw themselves move up the depth chart without doing all that much except making it through practice and not throwing up on Royal when he came down from the tower. "That was one of the most difficult times I have ever, ever had," Ted Koy, eventually the cocaptain and starting right halfback for the 1969 team, says of the 1968 spring drills. "We would hit from the time we broke from calisthenics. Coach Royal was going to go the next year with the survivors."

James Street, a backup quarterback in 1967 as a sophomore, also was fortunate enough to miss the 1968 spring practices: He was pitching for the Longhorns baseball team, under first-year head coach Cliff Gustafson. Street came over to watch the football workouts and wince. He remembers Royal saying, "The circle's getting tighter, we're losing a lot of players, but the ones staying here want to play ball."

Yes, that was 1968, but it was crucial in the development of the 1969 team. Royal and the staff knew they had "the Worster Bunch"—featuring fullback Steve Worster—coming into their sophomore years for the 1968 season, to go with a holdover starting quarterback, Bill Bradley. The Texas coaches were pondering installing an offense that suited the prospects' talents and also took advantage of the skills of the upperclassmen survivors. The fact that the Longhorns didn't come up with the new offense until *after* spring ball was one indication that those workouts primarily were designed as a screening process. The survivors had the guts to stick around, and they weren't always the biggest and the most talented, but they had spunk and, in most cases, brains. Sometimes it seemed sane young men wouldn't have put up with the hell the Royal staff put them through, but they did, and he was going to take advantage of the thinning ranks.

After that cornerstone 1968 spring training, Royal told his new offensive coach, Emory Bellard: *come up with a scheme that takes advantage of what we're gonna have left.*

As a high school head coach, Bellard won Texas state championships at three different schools. After San Angelo High won the 1966 Class AAAA title under Bellard, he finally made the jump to the college game, joining Royal's staff as linebackers coach. Following the third 6–4 season, Royal reorganized his staff, making Bellard the offensive backfield coach—effectively the coordinator.

Bellard doodled and tinkered in his office for hours, pondering splits and formations and pitchouts and belly rides and quarterback improvisations. He was barely a year removed from coaching high school, yet he eventually went into the office of one of college football's legends and said: *this is what we should do.* Bellard suggested a four-man backfield, a variation of the full-house "T" formation with the fullback within arm's length of the quarterback, and the halfbacks a couple of yards back on each side. The "*T*" had become a "*Y*," and the basic triple-option play would start with the quarterback "riding" the ball in the fullback's belly before deciding—quickly—whether to more emphatically jam in a handoff, or pull the ball out and go down the line himself. Then the quarterback's second and third options would be to cut upfield himself or pitch out to the trailing halfback—the halfback who had started on the other side of the formation. The basic formation would call for a tight end on one side (the "strong" side), a split end on the other.

"It took some guts on his part to do it," Bellard says of Royal. "We got a bunch of guys together who had completed their eligibility who were in summer school to look at it. One time, I played quarterback, and another time I found one. I messed with it to see if the quarterback could do the things we were going to ask him to do, and I felt if I could do it, I knew darned well I could teach it to an athlete."

In late July, James Street got a call in his hometown of Longview. James, he was told, it might be a good idea to be back in Austin by August 1, so you can be a part of the first look at a new offense.

The introduction was low-key. "We were out there working out," Street says, "and they said, 'Let's set up here and see how this works, see what y'all think about this.'"

With the fullback so close, the quarterbacks—Bradley and Street—found it impossible to "ride" the fullback long enough to survey the defensive reaction. "Bradley and I kept saying we could do it," Street says, "but neither of us thought it would work. You just didn't have enough time."

After the coaches moved the fullback a yard farther back, the timing began to work. Street and Bradley discovered the offense wasn't complicated. All it required was intuitive and intelligent reaction on the fly and taking care of the ball.

The Longhorns had a terrific holdover halfback, Chris Gilbert, and putting *both* Steve Worster and Ted Koy—each previously listed as fullbacks—in the backfield with Bradley and Gilbert was an astute deployment of resources, not just a strategic wrinkle. The split end was going to be Charles "Cotton" Speyrer, a speedy sophomore from Port Arthur, Texas, who wasn't able to play freshman football because of shoulder surgery. He was a highly recruited running back in high school and wasn't sold on the position switch. "I thought that was a demotion because UT was notorious for not passing the ball," Speyrer says. "I had my head down a little bit." As it turned out, though, with the Longhorns overloaded with running-back talent, it was the best thing for Speyrer—and his future.

Royal considered the wishbone a "modernization" of the split T he rode into coaching and up the ranks. "You make it a triple option instead of a double option," Royal says. "It's kind of unique that the side you're running the ball to, you can leave two guys totally unblocked and turn them loose."

Indeed, that was revolutionary: The offense allowed the reactions of one or two unblocked defensive players to help determine the quarterback's decision. That freed an offensive lineman or two to charge and block elsewhere, going after linebackers or defensive backs.

There were variations, though: on counter options, the fullback went one way and the quarterback did a reverse pivot and headed the other. On simple power plays, the fullback led the way through the hole for the halfback, who took a handoff, or the halfback took a handoff from Street after the usual "belly" ride with Worster. Passes usually came off play-action fakes to the fullback, with Speyrer typically the primary receiver.

Bellard didn't even think the offense was revolutionary enough to give it a pretentious name. To him, it was a variation of the veer-option offense, using three running backs instead of two. He says the original name for the package was "right-left," which he thought emphasized that the triple-option principles could work to either side—meaning not just right and left, but also to either the split-end or tight-end side. To Bellard, that was "balance."

Bellard and the staff taught the system to the Longhorns in the fall of 1968. And as with all experiments, there were early problems that had to be worked out in games. Bradley struggled and lost the number-one quarterback job after the Longhorns tied Houston 20–20 in the 1968 opener (in front of the Houston writer Mickey Herskowitz, who coined the name "wishbone T" for the Texas offense), and then lost 31–22 to Texas Tech in the second game. In that Tech loss, Worster, Gilbert, and Koy combined for more than 300 yards on the ground, and Street replaced Bradley in the third quarter. Street was named the starter in the middle of the next week, while Bradley's handling of the demotion earned him the respect of his teammates. When the change seemed imminent, he broke the tension at practice by running pass patterns as a wide receiver, loosening the cord on his sweatpants, and allowing them to drop down in mid-route. Within two weeks, he was a full-time safety, where he almost immediately was one of the best at the position in the country.

What was going on here? Three straight four-loss seasons, an 0–1–1 start, a new offense, and a switch to an unproven quarterback? Was this time for panic, time for the assistant coaches to get their résumés ready or hope that Royal would get another job and take them with him if he got fired?

But then the Longhorns raced through the rest of the 1968 season undefeated, setting conference records for total offense, rushing yardage, and average points in conference games. Each week, as one of the senior leaders, Bradley would say something along the lines of: "Don't worry, boys, Rat'll get it done." ("Rat" being James Street, the little quarterback who replaced him.) The Longhorns beat Arkansas, finishing in a tie with the Razorbacks for the Southwest Conference title and going to the Cotton Bowl because of the head-to-head victory. Texas drilled Tennessee 36–13 in that game, finishing 9–1–1. Although Chris Gilbert's career was over, the Longhorns were certain their period of mediocrity had ended. And much of the optimism was based on the success of the wishbone, and on the records of the backs returning for 1969.

Peter Alfano, *The New York Times*

TEXAS COACH WINS IN LOW-KEY STYLE

In this profile of Texas coach Fred Akers in 1984, Peter Alfano of The New York Times *takes a closer look at the low-key leader of many successful Longhorn teams in the seventies and eighties.*

There are romantics who would like to envision Dallas as still being part of the Old West, where cowboy boots and 10-gallon hats were a necessity rather than fashion and where the bars were called saloons and someone would be tossed out the swinging doors before the day was over. Fred Akers, the Texas football coach, can identify with the problem of overcoming stereotypes.

His conservative, low-key approach has been called bland and boring. His urbane, businesslike manner may be a more accurate reflection of life in Dallas nowadays than cowboy boots and 10-gallon hats, but it doesn't conjure romantic images.

It is his low profile in an age of celebrity coaches that might have kept Texas from making a stronger challenge to Nebraska for number one in the news-agency ratings this season. The Longhorns, who are 11–0 entering the Cotton Bowl game Monday against Georgia (9–1–1), are ranked second by the Associated Press and by United Press International and third by the computer ratings of *The New York Times*, and yet they sometimes fail to inspire even their fans.

This is a team that has perhaps the best defensive unit in the country, but an offense that is run-oriented and unimaginative, thus maligned, despite having averaged 25 points per game. Jeff Leiding, the colorful senior linebacker who is not cut in the typical Longhorn mold, said of the offense: "We can't criticize them because they'll pout."

Injury Alters Approach

But it would be inaccurate to suggest that the Texas offense merely is a reflection of Akers's personality. When the highly recruited freshman running back Edwin Simmons was injured and forced to sit out the season, Akers did not have a focus for his attack. He has relied, instead, on three quarterbacks, playing them like hunches or to fit specific situations.

"I feel that Coach Akers is conservative, but if I was in his position, I'd be the same way," said Rick McIvor, the senior quarterback and the best passer, thus least used. "I would do things that work well and are sure things, too."

And McIvor, who hopes to play professionally, has been frustrated the most, spending nearly every game on the bench as Rob Moerschell and Todd Dodge ran the option offense. He regained some respectability, however, when he passed for four touchdowns in relief of Moerschell to help Texas overcome Texas A&M, 45–13, in its last regular-season game after trailing by 13–0.

That was more to the liking of the offense, especially the guard Kirk McJunkin, who told his counterpart, Doug Dawson, that last season was more satisfying even though the team was 9–3. "I didn't agree with him," Dawson said. "I think the bottom line is winning.

"I realize that Nebraska got the jump on us by playing that first game against Penn State and that they have a high-powered offense. But who cares if they score 84 points against Minnesota? Does that mean they can beat us? I know that on offense, no one thinks we're great, but we have scored, you know."

Georgia Conservative, Too
There are similiarities between Texas and Georgia that make them appear like mirror-image teams, which figures to make the Cotton Bowl a low-scoring and, perhaps, dull game.

Last February, when Herschel Walker left the Bulldogs after his junior year for the New Jersey Generals of the United States Football League, it was too late in the recruiting season for Coach Vince Dooley to replace him. Thus Georgia has relied on a formidable defense and a conservative, ball-control offense featuring three tailbacks and two quarterbacks.

The Bulldogs have been praised for having another excellent season. "When Herschel left, a lot of people expected us to regress back to 6–5," said the senior quarterback John Lastinger. "As a team, we were at the crossroads."

But in Texas, the fans and alumni have not been as appreciative of the Longhorns. They are a tough audience as Texas is another program in which perennial success is expected. Akers has a 66–16–1 record in seven seasons, has won three conference championships, and has been to seven bowl games. But what is mentioned over and over again is the fact that he has not had a team rated as the national champion.

In 1977, his first year, the Longhorns were 11–0 and ranked number one entering the Cotton Bowl, but were beaten by Notre

Dame, 38–10. The 11 victories were forgotten. Then in 1980 Texas was 7-5 and there was a movement to replace Akers. He had followed Darrell Royal as the coach. Royal was a legend in Texas and the athletic director who hired Akers. He cast a long shadow.

Now the coach is more secure and even caused some consternation in Texas recently when he was offered the head-coaching position at Arkansas, his alma mater, after Lou Holtz resigned under pressure. Akers talked to Frank Broyles, his former coach and the Razorbacks' athletic director out of courtesy, he said, and respect for the people in Arkansas.

There was speculation, however, that he was enjoying the anxiety that was created back on the Texas campus in Austin. Still, Akers said: "I don't need publicity, and I'm not looking for credit. I think I've earned it, and if people fail to recognize that, I just won't send them a Christmas card."

"Coach Akers is confident and more at ease the past couple of years," Dawson said. "He appeals to our common sense, and his strength is that the players realize how sincere he is."

He is a paradox. Clean-shaven and neatly groomed, Akers would not be out of place carrying a briefcase on Wall Street. But despite a low profile, he said he did not want the players to be caricatures of himself.

"I don't want a football team of players who are all alike," he said. "I want to draw from all their strengths. I do want them to be a team, however. The players understand that we aren't an offense or a defense but a team. If a boat sinks, both ends go down. The problem is one of the perils of specialization."

A Bit of Understanding

Some reporters expected Akers to discipline or scold Leiding when the linebacker was involved in an altercation in a Dallas nightclub last week. The player was struck on the forehead with a beer bottle wielded by a patron in what apparently was an unprovoked act. This is not the type of publicity that Texas solicits.

"But Jeff was one of several players on both teams who was there," Akers said. "They were encouraged to go and have a good time by the bowl people. What happened to him could have happened to anyone. I've been in those situations, too.

"Jeff is a good player and free spirit. He is a sharp young man and an excellent team player. I think his reputation exceeds his deeds, however."

Akers can be feisty, too. When he was 22 years old, he applied for a head coaching job at a high school and was told by the superintendent that he was too young. "I told him, 'I thought you wanted a football coach, not someone who fit an age bracket,'" he said. His brashness was rewarded as the superintendent invited him to an interview, and he was subsequently hired.

Basically, though, the side the players see is the quietly effective motivator who uses meditation as part of his pregame ritual to prepare the team. "I won't call it hypnosis because that would sound flaky," Dawson said. "But I've fallen asleep relaxing after hearing his soothing voice."

It is the Texas fans who will have to shout about their team.

Michael Hall, *Texas Monthly*

THE EYES OF TEXAS ARE UPON HIM

Mack Brown accomplished his goal of restoring the Longhorn's glory by capturing the 2005 national championship. Texas Monthly*'s Michael Hall wrote this feature on Brown on the eve of that championship season.*

"I like happy people," says Mack Brown, the head coach of the University of Texas football team. "I really do. And I like my staff, and I want positive people around. I don't want negative people around these kids. I tell 'em, 'If you don't like it here, leave. If you stay, be upbeat, positive. I want you to have some fun.'" Brown has a warm, honest face, with friendly eyes. At 54, he is 6' and in good shape. He looks like what Opie Taylor might have looked like all grown up if Ron Howard had kept his hair. On this March day in his office, he is wearing khakis, loafers, a white sports shirt dotted with little burnt-orange Longhorns, and an optimistic smile about his team's chances in 2005. But Brown is always optimistic. "This is the best coaching staff we've had," he says. The high school coaches' clinic he had put on earlier that month, he said then, was the "best clinic we've had." Even though that winter's recruiting class had failed to meet expectations, "really," he said at the time, "that's a good thing." A word he often uses is "fun." "This is a fun time," he'll say, or as he said about his players at spring practice, "It is fun to coach and fun to watch them right now."

Brown should be having fun. In his seven seasons at UT, he's done almost every single thing right. He has won 70 games and taken the 'Horns to seven bowl games, winning four of them, including January's thrilling Rose Bowl, where UT beat Michigan on a last-second field goal. Brown has the best winning percentage among 'Horns coaches since 1922; indeed, over the past nine years, no college football coach except Florida State's Bobby Bowden has won more games than Brown. He has scored several top recruiting classes, bringing the country's best talents into a clean, well-run program. And he's brought back the fans, the alumni, and the boosters who had become disenchanted with almost two decades of Longhorns pigskin mediocrity. Ticket sales went from $8.3 million in 1997, the season before he arrived, to $20 million last year, a season that saw the football team net $37.5 million overall. Brown has even made Bevo hip. After years of being out of style, UT is now the number-two university in the country in merchandising sales.

It's been a long time since so many people outside Texas bought orange T-shirts or cared so much about the 'Horns. And around the Forty Acres, Brown gets the credit. "He's the closest thing we've had to Darrell Royal since Darrell Royal," says Houston lawyer Joe Jamail, one of UT's biggest boosters. Athletics director DeLoss Dodds adds, "He's unified our folks, and he's put a new face on recruiting. And he's done it with class." To reward Brown, last year the administration paid him more than any other coach in the country—$3.6 million, a base salary of $2 million plus a $1.6 million gift for staying at the university. In December, UT gave him a raise, a 10-year contract worth a minimum of $26 million. Nobody begrudges Brown the money; he earns every penny. At least for 364 days and 21 hours a year.

It's those three missing hours that drive the faithful crazy. Every October the Longhorns travel to Dallas for their biggest game of the year, the annual Red River Shootout with archenemy Oklahoma. But for the past five years, the Sooners and their coach, Bob Stoops, have humiliated the 'Horns, blowing them out (63–14 in 2000) and shutting them out (12–0 in 2004). Not only are the defeats soul-destroying, they keep UT from winning the Big 12 South Division and, ultimately, from getting to a national championship game. For some 'Horns fans, the streak, as well as Brown's reputation for not being able to win other big games (he's 3–10 versus top 10 teams), stirs a deep worry. Maybe, this nagging thought goes, Brown isn't the chosen one, the one who will lead them back to championship glory. Maybe he's just a great recruiter, a great salesman, a charmer who goes after, in his words, "nice kids who graduate." A great guy, but not a great coach. Maybe he's not tough enough, fiery enough. Maybe he's too damn nice.

Brown, of course, has heard this before, and his reaction is just what fans have come to expect. "My first thought when I heard that," he told me in his soft Tennessee accent, "was 'What a great thing to say about somebody. Too nice.' If that's the worst thing anybody ever says about you when you go lay down to die, that's probably pretty good."

On April 2, the last day of the 'Horns' spring practice season, under the shade of four sprawling oak trees on a worn patch of grass just east of Darrell K Royal–Texas Memorial Stadium, a bunch of fanatics gathered to drink beer, eat barbecue, and talk UT football.

They were tailgaters, and they formed an island of orange in a sea of black asphalt, dozens of people wearing "Longhorns," "Texas," or "Rose Bowl Champions" T-shirts; their numbers would grow five-fold by the 7:00 kickoff of the annual UT spring game. Meat smoked in a pit, and three large coolers held Bud Light, Coke, and water. Two Longhorns flags flew in the breeze, as if there were any doubt who was encamped here.

A parked white van had its back doors open, revealing a TV showing a DVD of the Rose Bowl game played just three months earlier. Diane Walters sat in a chair watching the game, while Jerry Clark tended the meat on the grill and James Lyle wandered among clusters of fans, drinking beer and chatting. On screen, quarterback Vince Young threw short passes to his tight ends, and running back Cedric Benson pounded away at the line. Every time the camera cut to Brown on the sideline, he looked tense and worried, his face hard, his mouth turned down. He wasn't having fun. Even after Young ran for a touchdown, making the score 7–0, Brown looked as if he were down 30 points. Walters looked on in admiration. "He's the hardest-working coach in football," she said.

The other fans shared her stubborn pride in Brown as a moral man in the violent, corrupt world of big-time college sports. "He has an open heart and embraces his coaches and players," said Clark. "The players desire to please him."

"When someone screws up at UT," said Walters, "the coaches go over to the kid and explain what he did wrong and why. They're teach-ers, not intimidators."

"It's not Mack Brown's job to yell at those kids," said Lyle.

"Brown made a conscious step to win," said Clark, "but with great players who are good students. The great Miami teams—the word that comes to mind is 'thug.' You'll never hear that term with UT and Mack Brown."

As the game progressed, fans would gather around the TV every time a big play was imminent. Most of them involved Young. A touchdown pass to tight end David Thomas in the second quarter. A 60-yard touchdown run in the third. Young is, everyone here agreed, the best college athlete in the country. He may have a strange, almost-girly throwing motion, but after two years, he's the most accurate passer in UT history, and he has the ability to freestyle his way through even the best defenses. "Next season lives and dies with Vince Young," said Walters. Young is the main reason the fans are excited about 2005, but they're also thrilled about new codefen-sive coordinator Gene Chizik, who last year led Auburn to one of the best defenses in the country. It's the offense, especially offensive coordinator Greg Davis, who has everyone worried. "He reminds me of a dog that chases parked cars," one of the tailgaters said. "He runs into one, falls down, gets back up. Runs into another, falls down, gets back up. How many times are you gonna do the same thing, especially in big games? Let's go play OU and shrivel up like a 10-year-old boy's testicles in cold water!" Everyone laughed. "We all agree," Clark said, "that in big games, Texas plays not to lose, instead of to win."

Early in the fourth quarter, UT was down 31–21 and had a third and goal on the Michigan 10. Walters announced, "Okay, ladies and gentlemen, this is the play." The crowd gathered around. Young took the ball, scampered back five yards, somehow spun his 6'5" frame to avoid a lineman, then slipped two more tackles and caromed into the end zone. "God," someone said. "It's just sick."

Young later scrambled for another touchdown, Michigan got a couple of field goals, and UT finally got the ball back with three minutes to go, down 37–35. Young marched the team methodically down the field, and Texas lined up for the winning field goal. I asked a couple of men if they were nervous, even though they knew what happened next. "Yeah!" they answered simultaneously. "All right, all right, all right!" Walters announced, flashing a hook 'em sign. The center snapped, kicker Dusty Mangum swung his leg, and the ball, barely tipped, wobbled over the goalpost. Everyone erupted in cheers, hopping up and down and giving high fives. Clark sat back down again. "How sweet the wine," he said.

The January victory was huge for both UT and Brown. Yet afterward, some fans still found reason to complain. UT had been ranked number six, they pointed out; Michigan was ranked number 12. The Longhorns were supposed to win. Also, it wasn't as though Brown had come up with some brilliant game plan; if any other college kid had been at quarterback, UT would have fallen apart. And if some Wolverine had gotten just one knuckle more on that kick, the Longhorn faithful would have wintered in despair.

But none of that mattered to the tailgaters. The Rose Bowl win had propelled Texas into 2005, the season in which many of them believe UT will beat OU (which graduated its Heisman-winning quarterback and many of its receivers and offensive linemen), and Mack Brown, the nicest guy in the meanest sport, will finally win the biggest game of all. "How many days until kickoff?" yelled Cody Norris, a late arrival. "One hundred and fifty-three? I'd rather chop off my big toe than wait that long."

Brown was hired away from the University of North Carolina in December 1997 for one reason: to bring a national championship back to Texas. He had a reputation as a "CEO coach," and he knew it wasn't enough to win on the field. Brown had to bring back the customers, improve the goodwill of the company. His to-do list looked something like this:

1. Call Coach Royal.
The new coach, who was born and raised in Cookeville, Tennessee, knew all about Royal, the last coach to win a championship for Texas, in 1970. Brown's father and grandfather were both high school football coaches, and they talked about the UT legend who was in his heyday in the late 1960s, when Brown was a star high school running back. When Brown was interviewed for the UT job, he asked Royal, who was part of the search committee, if he'd help him get the program back on its feet. Royal, who liked the confident, optimistic coach, said yes. He had been mostly ignored by his three successors, but Brown gave him an office and an open invitation to visit and accompany the team on road games. The new coach would even ask the old one to speak to the team. In return, Royal became Brown's mentor, giving him wisdom: "Football at Texas is every day," he said. "You're responsible for the way millions of Texans feel every day." It would be pressure like Brown had never felt. Royal also gave him comfort; both Brown's father and grandfather had recently died, and Royal would become a father figure. He also gave him cover; Royal would become a major ally when things went sour.

2. Reach out to fans, alumni, and the media.
The day after getting the job, Brown met with the media and more than 200 die-hard members of the Longhorn nation at the Frank Erwin Center, where he fired up the crowd by talking about playing a bold, high-scoring offense and a swarming, aggressive defense. Longhorns fans had heard about Brown: He ran an honest program and his players graduated. He was both emotional and smart. He was a hugger, known to cry after losing games, and he was a winner: an offensive coordinator at OU in 1984 under Barry Switzer (the best Switzer'd ever seen, the hated Sooner coach later said), a head coach at age 32 at Appalachian State, then Tulane, and then UNC, the basketball school that he took to 10–1 and number seven in the country, just before being hired at UT. After the Erwin Center pep talk, Brown hit the road, crossing the state and speaking to alums and fans at Longhorn Foundation meetings, telling stories and football anecdotes in the cadence of a politician; by football season he had given 93 speeches. The hungry Longhorn faithful packed the meetings and afterward met him, shook his

hand, and were thrilled that he looked them in the eye and remembered their names.

3. Make the players feel comfortable.
At the first team meeting, Brown joked with the players to stop ogling his wife, Sally, and he talked about having fun. "He came off really well," says former linebacker Anthony Hicks. "He struck us as different from [previous coach] John Mackovic— the way he would run the team. He [Mackovic] was aggressive and had an open personality. With Brown, I thought, 'This is gonna be fun.'" Brown did little things that meant a lot, like getting the team an air-conditioned bus for rides to the practice fields in the summer. He was, the athletes all agreed, a player's coach. He wasn't above fooling around with them, dropping down and doing push-ups, even dancing. And he was sincere. "He cares about you as an individual and as a player," says former linebacker Dusty Renfro, who played at UT from 1995 through 1998. "He wanted to make sure everything going on in your life was okay. He always took your side first—against other students, the administration—until he found information to change his mind. A lot of coaches are not like that." The player Brown needed the most that first season was running back Ricky Williams, who was contemplating leaving school early for the NFL. Brown persuaded him to stay for his senior year, and from that time on, he has not lost one player early to the pros.

4. Bond with high school coaches.
Texas has more blue-chippers than any other state, and Royal advised Brown that he needed to connect with the men who coached those boys. Brown and his new staff set out to visit every one of the 1,200 high schools where kids suit up in pads—and then stayed in touch with them. He started a high school coaches' clinic, where coaches could visit UT to learn how the big kids practice and play; it's now second in size only to the Texas High School Coaches Association clinic, attracting more than 1,000 coaches every March. Brown also invited the coaches to fall practices, which are usually off-limits to the rest of the world, and he gave them each a free pass to every home game. They came, they saw, they returned home excited about Brown, the UT facilities, and the Longhorns.

5. Bring back the lettermen.
Like Royal, former UT players felt underappreciated. Brown let them know they could visit his office anytime or come to

any practice. "That hadn't been done in recent years," says Ted Koy, star running back and member of the class of 1969. "He told us UT has a rich football tradition, and he wanted to cultivate it." Brown threw himself into helping with the yearly lettermen's golf tournament, and more and more former players began to show up. This April, 160 came, old-timers like T. Jones (class of 1959) and Koy, and more-recent grads like Hicks (1999). Most wore orange, and all had nothing but great things to say about Coach Brown. "He's brought back the family feel," says Hicks, "the orange blood, so people can say, 'This is Texas.'"

6. Recruit as though your job depends on it.
Brown almost immediately started knocking on the doors of high school phenoms. Recruiting is all about persuading, and nobody persuades like Brown. "He could talk me into eating a ketchup popsicle," said Bay City, Texas, quarterback Beau Trahan, part of that first class of recruits in 1998. Brown routinely scored the country's top prospects, such as New Jersey quarterback Chris Simms in 1998 and Midland, Texas, running back Cedric Benson in 2000. "Coach Brown just makes you feel like you've been friends with him your whole life," said Simms, now a quarterback with the Tampa Bay Buccaneers (Benson was the recent number-one draft pick of the Chicago Bears). To lure players, Brown also set to work upgrading UT's facilities. The 70,000-square-foot indoor space [the Indoor Practice Facility], a.k.a. the Bubble, was built. He remodeled the Moncrief-Neuhaus Athletics Center into a huge state-of-the-art facility. He installed a trophy room, where he encouraged visiting prospects to hold the Outlands or the Heismans of the past. He expanded the weight room. He took the kids down the hall past photos he'd put up: Longhorn All-Americans and academic All-Americans, great moments in UT history, and a wall of NFL helmets with the names of the 'Horns who had played for each team. He took the kids and their parents to the athletic facility's academic center, with its 36 computers, and told them that UT spends more than any other university on counselors and tutors for its athletes. And, he can now say, it works. When the NCAA released its first-ever academic report cards in February, UT passed, scoring higher than OU.

Royal—check. Fans, alumni, and media—check. Players, coaches, lettermen, high school kids—check. By the start of Brown's first season, his to-do list was done. That year the 'Horns went 9–3, with Williams running wild and winning the Heisman. Enthusiastic fans packed Memorial Stadium again, and by the time UT won the Cotton Bowl, Brown was a local hero. He'd go out to restaurants and people would stare or ask questions about the team or ask for autographs. Brown would politely answer and sign. After the season, his salary was increased to $1 million a year.

But his honeymoon with Texas fans lasted only until the 2000 OU game, when the Sooners crushed the 'Horns 63–14. Fans couldn't understand why Brown alternated quarterbacks, going from the freshman Simms to junior Major Applewhite, who had been the Big 12 Co-Offensive Player of the Year in 1999. Brown apologized to fans, coaches, and players afterward, calling it the worst loss of his career. He was lambasted for indecisiveness and playing it safe. What good is a great recruiter, asked some critics, if he can't coach those kids to win? Things didn't get much better the next year, when he again juggled the two quarterbacks, starting Simms but eventually replacing him with Applewhite in the Big 12 championship game, which UT lost. Still, UT went 11–2 and wound up ranked number five—the first time that had happened since 1983. In 2002 the 'Horns again went 11–2 and wound up number six.

The 2003 season ended terribly, when heavily favored UT lost to Washington State in the Holiday Bowl. Brown panicked, critics said, yanking then-freshman Young for the less-mobile Chance Mock against a team that was number one in the country in quarterback sacks. The loss gave more ammo to newspaper writers, talk radio callers, and angry posters on message boards such as the newly created firemackbrown.com. Yes, Brown was winning games against teams like North Texas. But he couldn't beat OU, and he couldn't win a conference championship, much less a national championship. He couldn't even get to a bowl championship series game.

Brown's UT office is a long way from the dank, cinder-block fieldhouses of his youth. The room, with dark paneling and white carpet, is large and heavy with a sense of accomplishment. Everything is orderly, and every artifact of glory is in its place: Heisman, Doak Walker, and Rose Bowl trophies on the coffee table; pennants, plaques, and group photos of teams past on the wall. Brown sat with his back to a huge window, through which you could see the grand expanse of Memorial Stadium. I asked him how he saw his job as head coach. "I'm in charge of a huge business with 130 student athletes, plus another 47 people who work in football in the building. And then there's your investment with the media, your fan support, your faculty. It does get enormous. You've got to be able to walk out of Joe Jamail's office with a coat and tie on and go into a high school with blue jeans that's maybe five miles away and then go into a 16-year-old's home that night. And handle all three situations well."

Indeed, the best college football coaches are multitasking geniuses: part motivator, part psychologist, part salesman, and part football brainiac. Brown was born and raised for the role. His father, Melvin Brown, was the tougher of his coaching influences. Once, as a Little Leaguer, Mack took a called third strike, and Melvin, watching with other parents, yanked him from the game. His grandfather Eddie "Jelly" Watson was gentler, yet still won more games than any other high school coach in Middle Tennessee history. Mack was brought up in a disciplined Church of Christ household, went to American Legion Boys State, sang in a choir, and played sports. He loved football most of all and got a scholarship to Vanderbilt, then transferred to Florida State, where, after his fifth knee operation, he gave up playing and began coaching. By the time he got to UNC, he had developed many of the things that make him the coach he is today, such as good-old-boy charm, an openness to others' ideas, and the ability to sell his own. He likes to talk, often quoting Royal ("As Coach Royal says, 'You don't ever want to sit in the shade.'") and spinning football anecdotes and aphorisms, many of which he's told before.

I asked him about the perception that he is a CEO coach. "I would think it's a compliment if it means I'm in charge of a corporation that has a huge budget and is a great source of revenue and attention for the university," he said. "If it means I don't do anything but delegate, I'd say it's an insult." Brown acknowledges that he spends a lot of time trying to figure out the right thing to do, collaborating with the people whose opinions he trusts the most—his assistants—then making the final decision. "Even my wife tells me I listen too much. I listen to a lot of people's opinions because I want to get their ideas. I'm gonna get all of those ideas because I feel I can make the decision a lot better if I know how our players and coaches feel."

When Brown arrived at UT, he found that his way was different from his predecessor's. "Mackovic was a micromanager," says former center Matt Anderson, who played for both men. "He'd watch the offense, critiquing everything, talking with players and coaches during and after practice. Brown lets his assistants coach. They're the ones who interact with the players every day. I'd much rather have the offensive line coach talking to me on the field." This doesn't mean Brown won't occasionally get down in the trenches with his players; at any given practice you will see him yelling, gesturing, and talking to his players face-to-face. "He's all about execution," says Hicks. "Run, block, catch, hit the runner. He makes the game simple."

On the field and off, nobody works harder. Brown gets to the office at 7:00 and sometimes doesn't leave until 7:00—and then he often has to attend some UT function. He puts his players through intense, regimented workouts, but he also treats them with respect. They say his door is always open, and when they come in, he asks them about their family or school. "He always talks about academics and the importance of graduating," says Rodrigue Wright, a senior lineman who could have been a first-round NFL pick this year but chose to stay and play his last year for Brown. "He always says that even if you do make the NFL, there's only two or three years in the league on average, and you have to have something to do afterward." Many of his players grew up in single-parent homes, and Brown, the son of a coach, becomes something of a father figure, often taking them to his home, where Sally will cook them dinner (the couple's four children are grown and gone). "We look up to him," says Young. "He makes us be better men—shows us how to treat our moms and girlfriends—when we see how he is with his wife. He shows you how to respect the adults around you."

Brown wants his players to be happy, and he wants them to feel good about themselves. "We never have 'weaknesses,'" he told me. "We have 'areas of concern.'" He sits down with each player at the end of the year and talks about what just happened and what will happen next. He seems to be at his best one on one, as he showed near the end of the Rose Bowl. Just before the final field-goal attempt, Michigan called a second timeout to try to ice Longhorns kicker Mangum, who trotted over to the sideline to talk to Brown. The TV cameras caught the brief conversation between the 21-year-old walk-on with more pressure on him than any Longhorn in modern history and his head coach, who had looked so intense and uptight throughout the game. With millions watching and their professional and personal lives depending on it, Brown laughed and joked and Mangum smiled and relaxed. Then Mangum went back out and kicked a football 111 feet through a space no wider than a Cadillac.

A UT alum I know has season tickets to Longhorns football games and last year took his entire family to Pasadena for the Rose Bowl. But he's stopped driving to Dallas for the Red River Shootout. He just can't bear the pain anymore, on the field—189–54 over the past five years—or off, where Sooners fans young and old taunt him and his family. Jeff Ward, an All-American place-kicker at UT in the 1980s and now an Austin talk-radio host, says, "A fan knows that something is going on: 63–14. Something's wrong. Something seems to paralyze the Longhorns on that day."

Depending on whom you ask, that something is either Mack Brown or OU coach Bob Stoops. Stoops is a defensive whiz who has devised elaborate schemes that confuse the 'Horns' offenses (and almost everyone else's) while he has allowed his backs to run wild. He's brash and arrogant. He gambles. In 2001, OU had a 7–3 lead and a fourth down on UT's 24-yard line with two minutes left. The Sooners lined up for a field goal, but Stoops had his kicker pooch a short punt, which put the ball inside the 5. On the 'Horns' next play, Stoops ordered a blitz; the safety hit Simms as he threw, and the ball was intercepted for a touchdown. Final: 14–3. In 2002, OU, down by 11, had a fourth and four on the UT 8 with 22 seconds left in the first half. Instead of taking the sure three points, Stoops went for a touchdown, got it, then went for the two-point conversion and got it, too. Now he was down by only three. UT got the ball back at midfield with five seconds left, enough time for one long heave into the end zone. But the 'Horns played it safe and ran out the clock. The Sooners went into the locker room with momentum and won, 35–24.

"When I hear Stoops," says my UT alum friend, "I hear enthusiasm. OU has cockiness and arrogance. It's real. Right now, OU expects to win. We hope to." Stoops's players know their coach is 12–3 against top 10 teams. They know he'll take risks when he has to. Dean Blevins, a former Sooners quarterback and the sports director for KWTV in Oklahoma City, says, "Stoops knows that the key thing is, the players have to trust him. They have to believe in him, especially at crunch time. The players will see a coach's body language and know his track record at crunch time. No excuses, an aggressive approach, and firm decisions. Stoops is the antipolitician."

Brown, meanwhile, has a woeful record against top 10 teams. Critics say that's because he plays it safe. Last year's 12–0 shutout, the first suffered by UT in 24 years, was a blueprint for fans' frustrations: a timid team, so nervous about making mistakes that it didn't go for it. The offensive game plan, used to great effect in September against the University of North Texas and Rice, was simple: give the ball to Benson and throw short passes, mostly to the tight ends. It was also predictable. Young wasn't throwing the ball downfield, so OU, which had a porous defense that was later torched by the University of Southern California in the national championship game, was able to put as many as nine men at the line, stuffing Benson and harassing and confusing Young to his worst game ever; he [Young] looked, some observers thought, as if he hadn't had any coaching. The receivers were too young and green to depend on, said Brown and offensive coordinator Davis later, though there had been plenty of practices and games against lesser teams to get them some experience. When Benson won the Doak Walker Award in February, he said publicly what many 'Horns fans have said privately about the OU game. "The coaches coach more of not to lose instead of trying to win," he said, adding that they need to "come up with a good game plan."

UT fans blame Davis, even though, in several of his years at UT, the offense has set yardage and scoring records. The coordinator is 54 and looks like a friendly banker, with a soft face and bifocals. He is, Brown says, an easy target: "Every school of this magnitude has an offensive coordinator who 90 percent of the fans are mad at. Every time a team loses, fans want the offensive coordinator fired. It's pretty predictable. The reason Greg has drawn so much criticism is we haven't scored points against OU. We haven't beaten OU." Brown, as the head coach, knows he must ultimately take responsibility for the offense. And the losing streak. "No doubt about it, the five losses to OU have been the negative thing we've done. The seed of any criticism of us comes from that game, and that's fair. It's the only thing keeping us from winning the national championship."

It's also costing them top recruits. In the stands at the 2003 65–13 horror was a kid from Palestine named Adrian Peterson, the best high school running back in the country, a Longhorns fan who had a poster of Ricky Williams in his bedroom. He hadn't been sure where he was going to college, but this game made up his mind. He chose OU, he said later, because the Sooners did a better job of developing players. He added, "One thing that has always bothered me about Texas is they can't win the big game. I like the odds with Oklahoma for winning a national championship." In last year's Red River Shootout, the Sooners freshman ran for an astounding 225 yards. Grand Prairie, Texas's Rhett Bomar, the best high school quarterback prospect in the country, also chose OU in the wake of the 2003 game. When he signed, he said how, in one meeting with Brown, the coach "wouldn't stop hugging me. He was such a nice guy. But in the end that stuff didn't make too much difference." What did matter was that OU and Bob Stoops seemed to be more serious about winning. Blevins says, "The perception of OU fans is that if Bob and Mack brushed against each other in a hallway, Bob would turn around with his fists up, and Mack would turn around and say, 'Excuse me.' Mack is the kind of guy you meet and think within two minutes, 'What a great guy.' But sometimes you can be too nice."

Every October, before the OU game, stories appear in the press and on talk radio about how Brown is on the hot seat, that he or Davis will be fired if UT loses again. And every year OU wins and nothing happens. Boosters like Jamail, brass like Dodds, and patriarchs like Royal say that the program is in the best shape it's ever been. It's winning, the blue-chippers are coming, the fans are back, and so is the money. According to Dodds, before Brown's debut season, UT had rented half of its 14 luxury suites; now there are 66 (at up to $88,000 a year each), and there are 200 names on the waiting list. Boosters gave $6.6 million to the Longhorn Foundation in 1997; last year they gave $18 million, and most of that came from die-hard football fans. "Mack is not on the hot seat and he's never going to be on it," says Dodds. "I have a tendency to dwell on the kids he has and the program he runs." Yes, it's important to beat OU, the optimists say, but the game has always run in cycles; many point to Nebraska's Tom Osborne, who lost to OU for five straight years then turned everything around and went on to win three national championships in the 1990s.

Jamail just laughs at the idea of a hot seat: "He's on such a hot seat we gave him a raise." The $26 million contract was approved before the Rose Bowl victory, without Brown's ever even winning the Big 12, and shows how much the UT bigwigs love him and, maybe, how little it matters whether the 'Horns win a championship under Brown. If Brown goes 10–1 for the next 10 years, I asked Dodds, and that "one" is OU, is that just the way it is?

"That's just the way it is," he said.

At around 6:30, the tailgaters began wandering over to the stadium for the spring game. All of a sudden it felt like fall. Forty thousand fans, mostly in orange, cheered as the players, in full uniforms, blasted through a cloud of dry ice. The Longhorns cheerleaders led the crowd in "Texas Fight!" and in the bleachers, five shirtless men stood next to one another with the letters *T, E, X, A,* and *S* painted on their chests, bellowing in the cool 55-degree air. Boosters sat in their luxury suites up high. Lettermen such as Derrick Johnson, a first-round pick in the recent NFL draft, stood in the grass behind the end zone.

In the hour-long scrimmage, Young threw some beautiful passes, tailback Ramonce Taylor ran back a kick for a touchdown, and tight end David Thomas made a spectacular leaping catch and somersault. The crowd roared. Brown stayed on the field for most of the game, the only coach out there (everyone else watched from the sidelines), standing about 20 feet behind Young. While Davis and his staff sent in plays and Gene Chizik and his people sent in adjustments and schemes, the head coach clapped, shouted encouragement, and blew his whistle. Sometimes he gave his players advice man-to-man, such as when he approached wide receiver Limas Sweed, talking to him and rolling his hands forward like a paddle wheel. He patted Young on the butt and once put his arm around his waist as they listened to something being shouted from the sideline. At the end, he gathered his players, said a few words, and they turned to face the crowd, holding up hook 'em signs as the band struck up the opening bars of the orange bloods' peculiar anthem: "The eyes of Texas are upon you/All the livelong day./The eyes of Texas are upon you/You cannot get away."

A few days before the game, Brown admitted that he didn't realize when he was hired in 1997 just how intense the scrutiny would be. He didn't realize that "every day" really meant every day. It took time, he said, but he learned to deal with it. His skin got thicker. He realized it wasn't about him; it was about the office he occupied. All he could do was his best, and when in doubt, he'd do what he felt was right, no matter how long it took to figure that out. If Brown has a mantra, he told me, it's this: "Stay fair to yourself." When I asked what he meant by that, he finally dropped the familiar quotes, anecdotes, and lines that sounded like they'd been used hundreds of times in front of thousands of boosters. "I didn't know for a long time who I was," he said, "and I didn't know that I didn't know who I was, but I was very uncomfortable at times because I kept fighting this something to prove to myself and everybody else I could do whatever this was. I wasn't sure I could do it. I still don't know for sure where all that comes from. If I sat down with a psychiatrist, he might say, 'Your dad jumped you as a Little League baseball player, so you had to prove it to him.' I don't know."

He paused, unsure for a moment where to turn. Then, quickly, he said, "But over the last—probably since we've been at Texas, really, I've been having more fun than I've ever had in my life."

With a national championship in 2005, thanks in great part to head coach Mack Brown, Texas football is where it was during the glorious Royal years.

Section IV
THE MYSTIQUE

Gary Shaw, *Meat on the Hoof*

THE GAME

One of the most controversial books ever written about college football was Gary Shaw's Meat on the Hoof, *an exposé of the University of Texas program under Darrell Royal. Shaw, a reserve lineman at Texas in the mid-1960s, had many harsh observations about playing for Royal. In this chapter from his book, Shaw takes the reader down on the field for the 1965 Oklahoma game.*

We were number one. Oklahoma would try to take it from us. Coach Royal is grim as he always is before a game. Still 90 minutes before kickoff, but I'm already up.

I pull my orange-and-white jersey down hard and plant it between my legs. My helmet is polished, and there are longhorns pasted on its sides. As I fit my head behind its facial bars and stiff elastic, I stare in the mirror. My right hand is wrapped and I have one elbow pad on. My shoulder pads are so big they seem to push out against the locker-room walls. I keep jamming thoughts out of my mind and sit down to wait.

"Alright men."

I stand up on metal cleats and line up at the door.

I start down the ramp and can feel the broken rhythm of a hundred separate feet. The crowd hasn't seen us yet. But within moments there is a rapid ricochet of cleats, slapped asses, and cracking voices.

"Let's get those sons of bitches, 'Horns! Let's go!"

I feel I'm assaulting the sidelines, not just heading toward them. I'm already punishing the grass below me, and the noise above me is hard—a rock band trapped and out of control. And when the Texas cannon explodes, the "amps" are turned loose.

"Hit somebody! Hit somebody!"

Those crazy son-of-a-bitch Sooner players are halfway across the field waving their fists and shooting the bird.

TV cameras and 75,000 people, concrete and bands, fans and orange, cheerleaders and red panties, referees and loud numbers, furious coaches and chalked grass, public speakers and Royal's mouth...

Hit!—as I lined up for the kickoff, I was ready.

Seventy-five thousand people were on their feet and looking down. After the kickoff my first 10 steps were consumed by one thought: *don't screw up!* Past those 10 yards my entire focus was on looking for the ball-carrier. "Get that son-of-a-bitch—get him!"

I avoided my blocker and was the first man down the field. When I looked up, the ball had rolled out of the end zone. Leaving the field, I was slapping members of the first team and screaming, "Get 'em, 'Horns! Put it to 'em. Get their ass!" Reaching the sidelines, I was still in a frenzy, and I kept pacing and yelling for another five minutes. Finally, momentarily exhausted, I calmed down and began to play the role of a reserve lineman.

My reserve lineman role was only one of the many acted out on the sidelines. The most amazing thing about our games was how everything was done according to standard form. We knew how to act when we were ahead and how to act when we were behind. Within this general breakdown there were distinctions between starters and reserves, offense and defense, backs and linemen, coaches and trainers—and all those various roles were very predictable.

There were a few things that "Daddy D." was always doing during a game—chewing gum, pacing back and forth, licking his fingertips, and repeatedly saying to those of us not on the field, "Now, men, get back off the sidelines."

Otherwise, his behavior when we were ahead was noticeably different from his behavior when we were behind. (Tied games were responded to as losses.) When we were ahead, Royal would nearly always get a blade of grass to chew on. During this winning period, his look would be one of serious and earnest intent. His pacing wasn't nearly as fast as when we were losing, and he would often come to a standstill while putting his hands on his hips, as if strutting. When we were ahead, his directions to a player were technical, slow, and in a subdued tone.

When we were behind, Daddy D.'s rituals changed dramatically. For instance, if he wanted some player, he would whirl around and yell, "Smith! Smith!" When Smith rushed up to Royal's side, Daddy D. would yank him close, grabbing him under the top of the shoulder pads. With teeth clenched, he'd growl a play and hurl Smith toward the field. When Smith was called forward, he usually wasn't wearing his headgear, and he'd still be trying to get it on halfway across the field.

Also, while invariably increasing his pace, Royal would begin spitting periodically at the turf. Then, looking like a man with a million thoughts running through his head, he'd grab the headphones from the backup quarterback or an assistant coach.

The players' form was just as predictable. When first-teamers came off the field winning, they sat down on the benches and threw their helmets between their legs. Then while all the also-rans came over and slapped congratulations, the first-teamers would begin giving orders to everyone around them. While ahead, they sat individually, chewed on ice and drank some saline solution (we always called it green shit). Periodically someone would be hollering at the trainer, "Trainer, bring me some of that green shit." The offensive backs would be the only ones who moved a great deal. They were the showboats and would walk from one end of the bench to the other, helmets off and sure to be in full view. They also seemed the ones most conscious of the fans when running off the field. If one of them had made a long run and was being replaced, he'd take his time before heading toward the sidelines. Players in the huddle almost invariably see a substitute coming in, and there is little question about whom he is replacing. But if a back waited until he was officially told in the huddle, he would then be able to enjoy his applause to a solitary exit. And once to the sidelines, he could occasionally hear people call down from the stands, "Great run, Joe!" The offensive backs would also be the only ones to walk over to get their own saline. And while they were walking by, we reserves congratulated them more than anyone else. "Great run, Helms!"

"Yow, we're pushing their ass all over the field," [J. A.] Helms would say.

The offensive line was usually the most humble group. They would throw their helmets down, rest their heads in their hands, and look weary.

But when we were behind, everyone looked more tired. We didn't shout as loud, but were more earnest. The defense would then get together and talk in a circle off to the side. The side chosen was always the one nearest to the game action. The offensive line would kneel anxiously on the sidelines, trading pep talk, whereas the quarterback and a couple of the backs would be crowded around Royal.

During the whole game (whether ahead or behind), [Frank] Medina would be racing back and forth giving his Medina lectures. But it was when we were behind that Frank became most vocal. He would go around slapping asses and talking to each starter individually.

"You can do it, men. You can do it! Now's the time to do it. Show 'em you're champions. Show 'em you're champions. Now's the time, men."

Yet when Frank was giving his individual speeches, he made sure to stay well behind the coaches.

For a reserve, the most important thing to do was to act ever ready.

"Keep your mind on the game at all times. Know the down and situation. You never know when you will be called."

Periodically a reserve's attention might stray from the action on the field to the girls in the stands. But he had to beware that a coach didn't catch him looking away from the game.

Most of the time the reserves tried to keep up a steady chatter of encouragement. The encouragement was usually a combination of fake enthusiasm and wishful thinking.

Our remarks about the game were generally criticisms of various starters' performances. If a guy we didn't like was screwing up, we'd say, "Smith is really fuckin' up. They're running all over his ass." If it was someone we liked, we'd sympathize. "Boy, John's having a rough time out there today—must really be tough."

For most of the reserves the scary thing was to be called in suddenly without warning. It doesn't give you time to get your psyche up.

That happened to me in the fourth quarter—with us ahead 19–0. Yet once I was out there, there was no fear of hitting or getting hurt. Instead, my only feeling was apprehension about performing well. I was playing defensive tackle. On the second play I helped throw the ball carrier for a three-yard loss, and I was suddenly conscious of the stands. The noise was a loud buzzing sound of approval. I felt on display, and I wanted to throw the quarterback for a huge loss. The next play, the defense came out of the game.

Heading for the showers, I felt tougher and meaner than I had before the game—even though I'd played only briefly. As I entered the locker room I remember thinking, I'm going to be a mean son-of-a-bitch by next year. I smiled at the thought.

Once in the dressing room, Royal gave us a brief talk (he always did this before reporters or others came in). We showered, picked up the box lunch in our lockers—fried chicken, Coke, and a big red apple—and then went to meet girlfriends and fans. As we swaggered out we would try to look humble.

I remember thinking, on the way back to Austin, how much simpler it seemed to put everything into football. Trying to get into other activities like the Tejas Club was merely frustrating. Finally, as we reached Austin, I said to myself, "To hell with all that other shit, I'm concentrating on football. I'm going to be a starter by spring training."

Ten days after the Oklahoma game, I hurt my leg and was out for the season.

Now I was left in my new surroundings of the Tejas Club without a chance to prove myself in football until spring.

Willie Morris, *Southern Living*

TEXAS-OKLAHOMA: LIKE THE CLASH OF ARMIES

The late Willie Morris, an exceptional editor and writer of such works as North Toward Home *and* My Dog Skip, *and a Texas alum, turned his attention to the Oklahoma-Texas rivalry in this 1988 article from* Southern Living *magazine.*

I remember as vividly as yesterday my pilgrimages as a University of Texas undergraduate in the 1950s to the Texas-Oklahoma football games in Dallas. I was a small-town boy from Mississippi, and there was an aura to those long-ago October weekends that seemed to epitomize, in my Thomas Wolfean adolescence, just what it was and how it felt to be young and vaguely innocent and *collegiate* in that day and place—the long drive north out of Austin on old U.S. 81 with one's favorite coed, the parties on Friday night in the Baker Hotel, where I found myself enveloped by the twangy Southwestern accents and the palpable affluence so foreign to my Deep Southern boyhood, the raucous midnight mobs at Commerce and Akard, the roar from the state-fair midway encompassing the Cotton Bowl on the golden Saturday afternoons, and finally the games themselves, which resembled the clashes of contemporary armies and had the flow of history behind them.

That was three decades ago, and over the years no American intercollegiate football rivalry has quite matched Texas-OU in its histrionic sweep. It is more than a mere event: it represents American society at its ultimate modern edge—violent, flamboyant, unpredictable, and withal somewhat self-righteous.

The two competitors have been playing since the start of the century. The site itself is almost exactly 200 miles from both Austin and Norman, and the game has been performed to sellout crowds for more than 40 consecutive years—75,587 will always be the official figure. Darrell Royal, the former Longhorn coach who participated in four of these games (as an Oklahoma Sooner) and coached in 20, claims that the Texas-OU rivalry exhausted him of much of his youth. "It's strange

150

how you can go down that ramp in perfect health," he says, "then a few minutes later actually be physically hurting just from making decisions on the sidelines. Every play is so vital, every foot of Astroturf. A fumble, an interception. One soft block and a yard less gained—that can be the difference."

All this is compounded, of course, by the heavy wagering that takes place every year between the oilmen of the two states, the blustery challenges and taunts and innuendos. My old comrade Gary "Jap" Cartwright, the Texas writer who once threw up on the Michigan State coach Duffy Daugherty in the course of an interview, is something of a cultural historian of the Texas-OU contretemps. (Because he attended TCU, he avows neutrality, rather in the mode of the Swiss Red Cross.) Jap discerns a deeper and perhaps more ominous significance in the rivalry. Oil and football, he contends, shape the characters of the two universities, and to a degree the states. "Texas and Oklahoma are neighbors only by a quirk of geography," he says. "They are separated by the Red River, which used to separate New France from New Spain. What really separates them is a century and a half of history, the Alamo as opposed to the Dust Bowl. When you hear a Texan or an Oklahoman call the other *neighbor*, it just means they share ownership in an oil well. They are like tribes connected by a common hatred, two people who look on one another with the special loathing usually reserved for cannibalism."

As part of this ineluctable tradition, it is not easy for either side to forget the special mayhem of 1967, known colloquially in Dallas as "the Night It Rained Furniture." As always, thousands of Texans and Oklahomans congregated in downtown Dallas in mad bacchanalia the night before the game. People were throwing beer all over one another. A bonfire went up on the street between the Baker and Adolphus Hotels. That was when the furniture started falling out of a 10th-floor window, chairs and desks and other paraphernalia that crashed onto the street near the rival crowds, tossed out by anonymous misbegotten souls. The Dallas police took in 500 of the more visible transgressors that night.

The two universities themselves—Texas with its nearly 48,000 students and Oklahoma with its 25,000—are among the richest in the nation and among the most aggressive in going after what they want. (UT, for instance, has a total of 975 endowed faculty positions and 71 chairs valued at $1 million or more each.) This academic competition suffuses the gridiron one in a cunning religiosity, and the animosity is exacerbated by the fact that some of Oklahoma's greatest All-Americans have been Texans, and that in any year the Oklahoma team prides itself on its substantial number of players from Texas.

In this formidable high-stakes drama, the Longhorns go into this October's match with a 47–31 margin in the series. Four have ended in ties, and the merchant princes and restaurateurs of Dallas complained that on these unsatisfying occasions both camps left town so quickly that business dropped to nothing.

It suggests much about the historic talent of these two football powers that there have been only four games since 1950 in which at least one of the two was not ranked in the country's top 10. During this time, on nine occasions one or the other went on to win the national championship. OU won six national titles in this period, Texas three. Thirteen times in the past 40 years one of the teams has gone into the game ranked number one. Oklahoma and Texas rank fourth and fifth, respectively, in all-time winning percentages in college football.

The most splendid of the Texas-OU games are chronicles in the memory of Longhorns and Sooners. Everyone will have a favorite.

1939: OU 24, Texas 12. The Longhorns' Cowboy Jack Crain, "the Nocona Nugget," scored from 72 yards twice within a span of a few minutes from almost the same spot on the field.

1947: Texas 34, OU 14. In Bud Wilkinson's first game against Texas, Sooner loyalists protested the officiating by throwing bottles onto the field. The referee needed a police escort, but before he left the stadium he knocked out an Oklahoma fan.

1950: OU 14, Texas 13. In Texas's only loss of the season, Billy Vessels ran over two defenders near the goal for the winning score.

1958: Texas 15, OU 14. Darrell Royal's favorite game, the first of eight in a row over his old mentor Wilkinson.

1962: Texas 9, Oklahoma 6. The Sooners' Lance Rentzel hitchhiked to the game from Norman and caught a long touchdown pass.

1968: Texas 26, OU 20. The Longhorns put together a 30-game winning streak and consecutive national championships.

1973: OU 52, Texas 13. Barry Switzer's first Texas game highlighted an undefeated season.

1976: Texas 6, OU 6. This acrimonious stalemate followed a week of accusations from Austin that Oklahoma coaches had spied on Texas practices. Royal and Switzer refused to shake hands, as if this or any other ceremonial amenity would have mattered at all.

The game itself has traditionally been integral to the State Fair of Texas. In addition to a 212' Ferris wheel, which is the same height as a

20-story building (and called by one Texan "the tallest damned Ferris wheel in North America"), this year's fair will feature a high-dive show, nocturnal parades, fireworks, a Broadway musical, fashion exhibits, and ice shows.

Yet it has forever been, in the thunderous magic of the Texas-OU game, the sights and sounds of the Cotton Bowl locale that have invested this storied rivalry with its grand and distinctive texture. It is these that will lay hard claim on the visitor in attendance there for the first time this October, just as they lay claim to my own heart now in youthful memory—this glittering Dallas skyline as seen from the stadium a couple of hours before the kickoff (surely the flawed and awesome American Dream writ large), the private planes and helicopters circling toward the airports on an azure horizon as a vignette from *Giant*, the visual splashes of the midway of the state fair all around. Inside the stadium there will be the vivid sea of orange and red when, at any given moment, exactly one half of the assemblage will be cheering, the world's largest bass drum in its burnt orange and white, the Sooner Schooner covered wagon pulled by its matching white ponies, the Longhorn steer Bevo gazing serenely at the mad scene before him, the resonant echoes of the bands from the end zones doing "Boomer Sooner" and "The Eyes of Texas." Surely the solitary and percipient archaeologist surveying this terrain a millennium or so hence will conclude: "There must have been some kind of public meeting place here."

Joe Drape, *The New York Times*

CHANGING THE FACE OF TEXAS FOOTBALL

The name Julius Whittier might not be as familiar as Earl Campbell, Cedric Benson, or Vince Young, but he helped pave the way for them and many others to star for the Longhorns. Shortly before Texas played for the national championship in January 2006, The New York Times' Joe Drape revisited Whittier's contributions to the program.

It was December 6, 1969, and Julius Whittier was stretched before a television in the lobby of the jocks' dorm, Jester Hall, when the euphoria of a heart-stopping victory lifted him, and most University of Texas students, [many of whom were] outside on Guadalupe Street. Texas had just beaten Arkansas, 15–14, in Fayetteville in what had been billed as the Game of the Century.

President Richard M. Nixon appeared in the locker room to declare the undefeated Longhorns as national champions. Whittier was a member of the Texas football team, but as a freshman he was not eligible to play varsity at the time.

He was also the only black football player at Texas. As Whittier pin-balled amid the revelers on the main drag here, he had an epiphany, one about the unifying elements within football that he would lean on for years.

"I had never experienced the exhilaration and joy of celebration where I was participating with what looked like millions of other kids my age," Whittier recalled recently at his law office in Dallas. "It did not matter that they were almost all white."

Neither Whittier nor anyone else knew that the time-capsule moment they were celebrating would become an inglorious mile-stone: the 1969 Longhorns were the last all-white team to win a national college football championship.

When Texas was conational champion with Nebraska the next year, Whittier was a backup offensive lineman and the Longhorns' first black letterman. He acknowledged that he had endured indignities, but said his life experiences were expanded as much as those of his white teammates.

By playing at Texas, Whittier received advice from former President Lyndon B. Johnson over lunch at his ranch and learned to love the music of Willie Nelson.

"I was a jock, plain and simple," he said. "I didn't care about civil rights or making a mark. I just wanted to play big-time football."

Whittier, however, is intensely interested in the January 4 Rose Bowl, the national title match-up between defending champion Southern California and Texas. He is proud that about half of the players on the Longhorns' roster are black, including the star quarterback Vince Young.

"It completes the circle from a team that had no blacks to a truly diverse one, one with a black athlete in the ultimate leadership position—quarterback—of the university's most prized institution," Whittier said.

William Henry Lewis was the first black player in major college football at Amherst from 1889 to 1891, then at Harvard from 1892 to 1893, when he was a law student. At the time, both teams played schedules of national prominence, according to the College Football Hall of Fame in South Bend, Indiana. Bill Willis, a tackle for the 1942 Ohio State Buckeyes, was the first black player on a national championship team.

In the South, however, all-white teams were the norm into the late 1960s as the region was slow to embrace civil rights, especially in something as cherished as college football. Jerry LeVias might have integrated the Southwest Conference in 1966 at Southern Methodist University, but on that December day in 1969 with Nixon in the stands, the top-ranked Longhorns were facing another all-white team in number-two Arkansas, a Southwest Conference rival.

"How's that song go?" said Darrell Royal, the Longhorns coach who won three national titles from 1957 to 1976. "Things they are a-changing. But they weren't changing that quickly around here at the time."

When Royal arrived here, he was 32 and fresh from head-coaching stints at the University of Washington and with the Edmonton Eskimos of the Canadian Football League. He had coached black players at both stops.

The University of Texas admitted black students in 1956, but did not lift its ban on their playing varsity sports until 1963. Even then, Royal acknowledged, there was tacit pressure from university regents for him not to rush to integrate the football team.

In 1967 Royal and his staff recruited a local star named Don Baylor, who was also a gifted baseball and basketball player. He grew up in

west Austin—knowing that downtown there were separate water foun-
tains for blacks and whites—had integrated his junior high school, and
dreamed of breaking the color barrier at Texas.

Baylor wanted to play all three sports, something universities like
Stanford, Oklahoma, and Texas Western would allow. Royal wanted
him to play only football. Baylor would not say that Royal and Texas
made a halfhearted attempt to lure him, but he said they were relieved
when the Baltimore Orioles drafted him.

"The Southwest Conference and UT was not ready to break the
color barrier," said Baylor, who had a distinguished 19-year Major
League career and later managed the Colorado Rockies and the
Chicago Cubs. "The Orioles took the pressure off Texas."

In the fall of 1968, Royal believed he had found the right young
man to integrate his team in Julius Whittier. The previous season, a
black student named E. A. Curry walked on and made the freshman
team, but he struggled academically and quit. Royal's first black scholarship player in 1968, Leon O'Neal, stayed for only one year.

Royal believed Whittier had the will and the preparation to remain
for four years. Whittier had been a star at an integrated high school in
San Antonio. His father, Oncy, was a doctor. His mother, Loraine, was
a schoolteacher and community activist who had led protests against
a local grocery chain that prohibited black women from becoming
cashiers.

Whittier said his uncle Edward Sprott was head of the NAACP in
Beaumont, Texas, and had not been intimidated when his house was
bombed. His older brother, also named Oncy, had his head cracked
open by police officers for his involvement in a guerrilla theater troupe
that performed pointed skits about prejudice in the streets of San
Antonio, Whittier said.

Royal described Whittier as "smart and tough and a heck of a football player." He added, "I knew he could play for us and handle any
difficulties off the field."

Whittier said he turned two personal flaws into powerful tools of
perseverance. He was not only confident to the point of cockiness, but
also had a gift for oratory that continues to serve him well as a trial
lawyer.

"I had a mouth that I ran a lot and coherently," he said. "It sounded
like I knew what I was saying, and that protected me."

Whittier also struggled with attention deficit disorder.

"It kept me so wrapped up in the events of each moment, class,
workout, dinner, study hall, practice, game, new friend I made, new
football play I learned, and each paper I had to turn in," he said. "I had
no real time or hard-drive space in my brain to step back and worry
over how potentially ominous it was to become a black member of the

University of Texas football team and all of the horrifying things that, from a historical perspective, could happen to black people who dare to accept a role in opening up historically white institutions."

Whittier recognized slights by teammates. He was never invited out drinking or to parties with his teammates. And though racial slurs were never directed at him, Whittier heard them when his fellow Longhorns forgot he was in the room.

Before Whittier's sophomore season, Royal had trouble finding him a roommate. He called in some of his seniors and explained the situation. One of them, running back Billy Dale, volunteered.

The year before, Dale scored the game-winning touchdown against Notre Dame in the Cotton Bowl to keep alive Texas's winning streak, which eventually reached 30 games. He was also among the most popular players on the team— until then.

"I lost all my friends," said Dale, now a manufacturer's representative in Austin. "I chose to live with Julius because I believed it would add that much more dimension to me as a person."

One night as the two readied for bed, Whittier engaged Dale in an argument about mortality.

"Billy, I'm never going to die," Whittier told Dale, "and you are."

The longer the exchange went, the more Dale became frustrated.

"I crossed the room and put a finger in Julius's eye and said, 'It's people like you who give your race a bad name,'" Dale recalled.

"You think, I'm serious, Billy?" Whittier responded with a smile. "I'm just trying to make you think."

They never exchanged cross words again.

It was Whittier's engaging personality that made him one of Royal's favorites and got him on Johnson's guest list. Johnson was crazy about Texas football and occasionally asked Royal to take players to his ranch. It was Johnson who suggested that Whittier continue his studies at the university's new school of public affairs. He earned a master's degree there, before he became a lawyer.

Whittier's success on and off the field—he was a three-year letterman and a starter his junior and senior year—paid immediate dividends for Texas. Roosevelt Leaks came here in 1971 and Earl Campbell in 1974, and they became All-American running backs. Soon, one of the set pieces for prospective players was Johnson's landing by helicopter on the lawn of his presidential library on campus to tell them why they should play for Texas.

Thirty-six years after Whittier watched his white teammates defeat Arkansas, much has changed in the Texas football program. Jester Hall remains, though it is no longer strictly an athletic dorm. Royal, now 81, remains a campus fixture, though one who concedes he could have been more aggressive in integrating his team earlier.

And Dale remains active in the Longhorns letterman association.

"All those people I had lost as friends by rooming with Julius are friends again," he said. "We've all grown."

Whittier, too, remains in touch with Royal. He now has a far easier relationship with his former teammates than he had when he was a college student. "When I see guys from my era, I feel a sense of comradeship," Whittier said. "I never was going to hold on to any of the bad stuff, and neither have they."

He will watch Vince Young and the number-two Longhorns try to upend the number-one Trojans from his couch at home in Dallas with the same anticipation and joy that he had as a pioneering Texas freshman. Whittier will root for another championship, another time-capsule moment, but one that will not be marred by a footnote about race. He is hoping his role in Texas football history is further diminished.

"You know that football is a religion in Texas," he said. "God and the university had the right people in the right places to handle my situation. It turned out to be a small event in the long and luminous life of a great and valuable institution."

Robert and Katy Agnor, hornfans.com

LONGHORN QUOTES

Enjoy the following quotes on various Texas football subjects down through the years, compiled by and originally appearing on hornfans.com.

"We're ready."
—DARRELL K. ROYAL IN PREGAME INTERVIEW
FOR JANUARY 1, 1964 COTTON BOWL

"Total domination. It's the only way to go."
—DUSTY RENFRO ON THE 1999 COTTON BOWL

"All the white meat is gone. There's nothin'
but necks on the platter."
—DARRELL K. ROYAL ON THE REST OF A TOUGH SCHEDULE
AFTER BEATING A COUPLE OF SOFT OPPONENTS

"He doesn't have to be spectacular,
we just want him to drive the car."
—OFFENSIVE COORDINATOR GREG DAVIS ON QUARTERBACK MAJOR
APPLEWHITE'S FIRST CAREER START

"That guy is a big ol' cuss…look at him rumblin' down the
field…looks like a grizzly bear haulin' a walnut."
—DARRELL K. ROYAL ON A BAYLOR TIGHT END

"I don't know. Never had one."
—DARRELL K. ROYAL TO MACK BROWN ON HOW
TO COACH A TEAM AFTER A LOSING SEASON

"Dance with the one that brung ya."
—DARRELL K. ROYAL

"Will Rogers never met Barry Switzer."
—DARRELL K. ROYAL

"Winning coaches must treat mistakes like copperheads in the bedclothes—avoid them with all the energy you can muster."
—DARRELL K. ROYAL

"Football doesn't build character. It eliminates the weak ones."
—DARRELL K. ROYAL

"Breaks balance out. The sun don't shine on the same ol' dog's rear end every day."
—DARRELL K. ROYAL

"Are you *sure*, Coach?"
—JAMES STREET, FAYETTEVILLE, 1969, FOURTH DOWN

"I called it. And I called it long."
—DARRELL ROYAL, FAYETTEVILLE, 1969, FOURTH AND THREE

"Come on, men, we've got'em where we want'em now. They've run out of room to pass. They've got to come right at us."
—LINEBACKER JOHNNY TREADWELL, 1962, AS ARKANSAS LINED UP ON THE 3-YARD LINE TRYING TO GO UP BY 10 POINTS (TREADWELL AND PAT CULPEPPER CAUSED ARKANSAS FB DANNY BRABHAM TO fumble, TEXAS RECOVERED, DROVE 85 YARDS, AND WON 7–3)

"When I was a kid and got in trouble, I'd always say, 'Mom, I'm in trouble.' Well, Mom, I'm in trouble."
—EARL CAMPBELL, TRYING TO FIND THE WORDS TO EXPRESS HIMSELF AFTER WINNING THE HEISMAN TROPHY, 1977

"He's not in my will or anything like that."
—FRED AKERS ON BARRY SWITZER, 1977

"I've been here five years, and we've won five championships. (Travis) Roach and I are going to write a book. We're going to call it *Five in a Row, or Cab Driver, One More Time Around the Block*."
—LINEBACKER RANDY BRABAND AFTER THE 'HORNS BEAT TCU 27–0 IN 1972 TO CLINCH TEXAS' FIFTH-STRAIGHT SWC TITLE

"He's not very fast, but maybe Elizabeth Taylor can't sing."
—DARRELL ROYAL ABOUT A SLOW PLAYER

"Punt returns will kill you quicker than a minnow can swim a dipper."
—DARRELL K. ROYAL

"You never lose a game if the opponent doesn't score."
—DARRELL K. ROYAL

"Get out the wide-angle lenses, boys, I'm gettin' ready to smile!"
—FRED AKERS

"We could never figure out why they didn't choose to settle it on the grass in Dallas, rather than from a soapbox in Pennsylvania."
—FREDDIE STEINMARK ON THE PROTESTATIONS OF PENN STATE AND JOE PATERNO THAT THEY DESERVED THE MNC IN 1969, AFTER THEY REFUSED THE INVITATION TO PLAY THE 'HORNS IN THE COTTON BOWL

"Luck is what happens when preparation meets opportunity."
—DARRELL K. ROYAL

"If worms carried pistols, birds wouldn't eat 'em."
—DARRELL K. ROYAL

"And that's why I decided to stay for my senior season."
—RICKY WILLIAMS

"Sometimes you have to suck it up and call a number."
—DARRELL K. ROYAL DESCRIBING 53 VEER PASS IN THE BIG SHOOTOUT

"Hey, by the way, tell [Lee] Corso I made
it through the game all right."
—RICKY WILLIAMS AFTER THE 1998 HUSKER GAME

"Ricky can't come back next year, I have already checked.
Oh yeah, he can't sing, either."
—MACK BROWN ON WHAT RICKY WILLIAMS CAN'T DO

"Three things can happen when you pass,
and two of 'em are bad."
—DARRELL K. ROYAL

"Nine in the box...that's a football term."
—RICKY WILLIAMS TO DAVID LETTERMAN

"If you can't get behind him, just get enough for the first
down. But if you can get behind him, run like hell."
—JAMES STREET TO RANDY PESCHEL IN THE HUDDLE ON FOURTH
AND THREE FROM THE 43 WITH 4:47 REMAINING IN THE
BIG SHOOTOUT, FAYETTEVILLE, 1969

"Maybe we'll beat *them* by 21 points!"
—JAMES BROWN PRIOR TO THE 1996 BIG 12 CHAMPIONSHIP
GAME (10 TURNED OUT TO BE ENOUGH)

"I like to watch Coach Campbell coach. Of all my
professors at the University of Texas, he knew
his field better than they knew theirs."
—DAN MAULDIN ON MIKE CAMPBELL

"Let them have their fun over there tonight.
After we finish what we came here to do, this town
will belong to us for the next three days."
—Texas coach Blair Cherry to the Longhorns on New Year's Eve, 1947,
when the 'Horns were in New Orleans to play Alabama—
the next day, Texas beat the Tide 27–7

"Once you cross the 50 you feel like an unsaddled horse."
—Darrell K. Royal

"He runs like a bucket full of minnows."
—Darrell K. Royal on James Saxton, 1961

"Boys! The eyes of Texas are upon you. Texans are huddled
around their radios from Brownsville to Wichita Falls, from
El Paso to Texarkana, in every home, grocery store, drug
store, barbershop, and hardware store in the state of
Texas—all are eagerly waiting to find out how you do
today. Today, you are not just representing the University
of Texas. Today you're fighting and playing for the entire
state of Texas! This is Texas against Wisconsin! Set your
jaws! Make up your minds! Let's play a game that will live
in the hearts and minds of the people of Texas *forever*!"
—Texas Coach D. X. Bible's pregame speech to the
Longhorns prior to the 1939 contest with Wisconsin that
Texas won 17–7 over the larger UW squad

"Hey, Looney, get off the field, you creep.
You're killin' the grass."
—UT's Bobby Gamblin to OU's Joe Don Looney in the
1963 Texas-OU game (Texas 28, OU 7)

"Roosevelt Leaks All Over the Field"
—Newspaper headline after Roosevelt Leaks ran for
342 yards versus SMU in 1973

"Randy, I'm talking to you. I'm looking at Cotton,
but I'm talking to you!"
—JAMES STREET TO RANDY PESCHEL (BUT POINTING AT COTTON
SPEYRER IN EMPHASIS) IN THE HUDDLE BEFORE THE FOURTH AND
THIRD PLAY AGAINST ARKANSAS IN 1969 (STREET HAD NOTICED THE
ARKANSAS PLAYERS LOOKING INTO THE HUDDLE ALL AFTERNOON)

"A boy shows how much he wants to play in the
spring when it's tough, and during two-a-days
when it's hot and tough. I don't count on the boy
who waits till October, when it's cool and fun, then
decides he wants to play. Maybe he's better than
three guys ahead of him, but I know those three
won't change their minds in the fourth quarter."
—DARRELL K. ROYAL

"Somebody get that idiot off the goalpost!"
—WALLY PRYOR, TEXAS VERSUS UH, 1990

"When Earl ran, snot flew. I haven't seen any snot fly yet."
—DARRELL K. ROYAL WHEN ASKED TO COMPARE BUTCH HADNOT
TO THE TYLER ROSE

"You just threw three balls at last year's
Texas high school high-jump champion."
—JERRY GRAY TO AN SMU QB WHO THREW THREE-STRAIGHT FADES IN THE
NORTH END ZONE AT FRESHMAN JAMES LOTT, WHO BROKE UP ALL THREE

"I don't know if Earl's in a class by himself,
but it sure don't take long to call roll."
—BUM PHILLIPS ON EARL CAMPBELL

"They're like a bunch of cockroaches.
It's not what they eat and tote off, it's what
they fall into and mess up that hurts."
—DARRELL K. ROYAL ON TCU

"Don't matter what they throw at us.
Only angry people win football games."
—Darrell K. Royal

"I had hoped God would be neutral."
—Darrell Royal on seeing a sign in front of a
church reading: "Darrell Royal, Cast not thy steers
before swine," before the 1969 Game of the Century

"Old ugly is better than old nothing."
—Darrell K. Royal

"You've got to think lucky. If you fall into a mud hole,
check your back pocket—you might have caught a fish."
—Darrell K. Royal

"It was like having a big ol' lollipop in your mouth, and
the first thing you know all you have is the stick."
—Darrell K. Royal on losing a game in the last minute

"Give me a guy with his jaw stuck out, his shirt sleeves
rolled up, and who swaggers when he walks. I know its
Harry High School, but if I have to make a choice, I'll take
the cocky, over-confident, conceited kid over the one who
has so much humility he can't look you in the eye."
—Darrell K. Royal

"If everything had already been done, there would be
nothing left for young people to accomplish. There are
always going to be people who run faster, jump higher,
dive deeper, and come up drier."
—Darrell K. Royal

"I'm going to learn it. You have to learn it up there.
It's like the Bible. I'm going to learn it."
—Rod Babers on "The Eyes of Texas"

"I decided on Texas because it is close to home.
It is close to my parents. And it's the State of Texas.
You don't know how much I love the state.
When we left and came back to Texas, I realized
how much I missed it. This is my home. It's been
in my heart. The state of Texas has been good to me.
And I want that to continue."
—CORY REDDING ON WHY HE CHOSE THE UNIVERSITY OF TEXAS

"A head coach is guided by this main objective: dig,
claw, wheedle, coax that fanatical effort out of the
players. You want them to play every Saturday
as if they were planting the flag on Iwo Jima."
—DARRELL K. ROYAL

"Hell no. I'm not going to candy this thing up.
These are work clothes."
—DARRELL K. ROYAL ON FANCY, STRIPED UNIFORMS

"Every coach likes those players who, like trained pigs,
will grin and jump right in the slop."
—DARRELL K. ROYAL

"You're what-iffing now, and everybody can what-if."
—DARRELL K. ROYAL

"He runs faster than small-town gossip."
—DARRELL K. ROYAL ON THE SPEED OF HALFBACK JAMES SAXTON

"The only thing that disturbs me about my profession
is the fact that people give you too much credit
when you win and too much criticism when
you lose. I'll be the same person and do the
same things and say the same things when we
lose. But people won't believe me then.
I won't change, but the people will."
—DARRELL K. ROYAL

"To say we were the only ones aggressive would be like a skunk telling an opossum his breath smells."
—DARRELL K. ROYAL

"When you get to the end zone, act like you've been there before."
—DARRELL K. ROYAL

"Just as happy as a gopher in soft dirt."
—DARRELL K. ROYAL, WHEN ASKED HOW HE FELT ABOUT BEATING NOTRE DAME IN THE SAME COTTON BOWL

"We would like to sign a punter. We'd rather not punt. But based on my experience, that happens some."
—MACK BROWN

"It's coming. It's right around the corner. Keep your eyes open because the state of Texas and the Longhorns are on the warpath, and we're making our way to a national championship."
—CORY REDDING

"We live one day at a time and scratch where it itches."
—DARRELL K. ROYAL

"There is no such thing as defeat except when it comes from within. As long as a person doesn't admit he is defeated, he is not defeated—he's just a little behind and isn't through fighting."
—DARRELL K. ROYAL

"Next to weather, there is no equalizer like two fired-up football teams."
—DARRELL K. ROYAL

"We're not exactly a rolling ball of butcher knives."
—DARRELL K. ROYAL

"The tail should never wag the dog, but as long as football is in its proper place on the campus, then it's good. I want to be remembered as a winning coach, but I also want to be remembered as an honest and ethical coach."
—DARRELL K. ROYAL

"One player was lost because he broke his nose. How do you go about getting a nose in condition for football?"
—DARRELL K. ROYAL, WHEN ASKED IF THE ABNORMAL NUMBER OF LONGHORN INJURIES THAT SEASON RESULTED FROM POOR PHYSICAL CONDITIONING

"You've got to be in a position for luck to happen. Luck doesn't go around looking for a stumblebum."
—DARRELL K. ROYAL

"He's smoother than smoke through a keyhole."
—DARRELL K. ROYAL

"They cut us up like boarding house pie. And that's real small pieces."
—DARRELL K. ROYAL

"We're just as average as everyday wash."
—DARRELL K. ROYAL

"When you're in elementary school, that's all anyone talks about—Pee Wee football and on and on. It's king in the state of Texas. Football is my life. It's just around me. Everybody I know, all my friends, they play football. That's what we do in Texas."
—B. J. JOHNSON

"So what if I'm tired? I can rest when I die."
—MAJOR APPLEWHITE

"Fat people don't offend me.
What offends me is losing with fat people."
—Darrell K. Royal

"Once the ball is in the air, it's mine. That's like $10
million floating in the air, and (a DB) is not going to get
$10 million from me. If Bevo was sitting on $10 million,
I would pick Bevo up to get the money."
—Roy Williams

"Once I get behind a DB, I act like he's a dog. I'm not
going to be caught by a dog. I don't like dogs."
—Roy Williams

"We have been in the neighborhood of the
top 10 a few times. What we need to do is
buy a house in that neighborhood."
—Mack Brown

"I plan to...give the Ags many headaches at
Kyle Field, and I have nothing to say to the Sooners.
They probably couldn't read it anyway."
—Rufus Harris

"Destructive back."
—Rufus Harris on what position he will play at UT

"Leadership is what you do when nobody is watching."
—Cory Redding

"Being a leader is just being you, not trying to be
someone else."
—Cory Redding

"Football's so important in Texas. On the West Coast,
it's a social. On the East Coast, it's a culture.
Here, it's a religion."
—MAJOR APPLEWHITE

"If you want to surf, move to Hawaii. If you like
to shop, move to New York. If you like acting
and Hollywood, move to California. But if you
like college football, move to Texas."
—RICKY WILLIAMS

"I'm like a heat-seeking missile,
and the ball carrier is my target."
—DERRICK JOHNSON

"There are only two sports in Texas:
football and spring football."
—FORMER TEXAS SPORTS INFORMATION DIRECTOR JONES RAMSEY

"I know that someday Texas A&M will
defeat the university in Memorial Stadium,
but I don't want that to happen to you boys."
—D. X. BIBLE TO THE TEAM BEFORE THE 1940 GAME

"I like to dominate, and frankly,
looking at me is a scary sight."
—LARRY DIBBLES

"First, Notre Dame has to lose."
—DARRELL K. ROYAL ON HOW TO WIN A NATIONAL CHAMPIONSHIP

"I could've juked him, but I just hadn't had
the chance to run over anybody in a long time."
—IVAN WILLIAMS REGARDING A HUSKER DB

"Hook 'em, Horns, and God Bless America."
—PRESIDENT GEORGE W. BUSH TO CLOSE AN ADDRESS
HONORING COACH DARRELL K. ROYAL AS THE INAUGURAL RECIPIENT
OF ESPN'S CONTRIBUTIONS TO COLLEGE FOOTBALL AWARD

"Nobody leaves this field until
we beat the hell out of them."
—L. J. "LOUIS" JORDAN IN 1913
BEFORE THE KICKOFF OF THE TEXAS-OU GAME

"He could talk me into eating a ketchup Popsicle."
—BEAU TRAHAN ON MACK BROWN

"My dream is to beat everybody by 50–60 points
and make 'em wish they hadn't played Texas."
—CHANCE MOCK

"If you like the hills and you like pretty ladies,
Austin is definitely the place to be."
—CHANCE MOCK

NOTES

The publisher has made every effort to determine the copyright holder for each piece in *Echoes of Texas Football.*

Reprinted courtesy of *The Sporting News*: "Roping Steers Won't Be Easy with Nobis Roaming the Range" by Bob St. John, copyright © September 18, 1965. Reprinted with permission; "Good Fella" by Kirk Bohls, copyright © August 17, 1998. Reprinted with permission; "Texas Two-Step" by Bill Minutaglio, copyright © September 11, 2000. Reprinted with permission; "Leapin' Longhorns" by Tom Dienhart, copyright © January 10, 2006. Reprinted with permission.

Reprinted courtesy of *The New York Times*: "Reserve Quarterback Puts Texas on Dream Street" by Neil Amdur, copyright ©1969 by The New York Times Co. Reprinted with permission; "Texas Coach Wins in Low-Key Style" by Peter Alfano, copyright ©1984 by The New York Times Co. Reprinted with permission; "Changing the Face of Texas Football" by Joe Draper, copyright © 2005 by the New York Times Co. Reprinted with permission.

Reprinted courtesy of *The Washington Post*: "Gilmer Failure as Rival Stars" by Shirley Povich, copyright © 1948 by *The Washington Post.* Reprinted with permission; "Longhorns Score Early, Win 28–7" by George Minot, copyright © 1963 by *The Washington Post.* Reprinted with permission.

Reprinted courtesy of the *Dallas Morning News*: "Field's 60-Yard Dash Beats Tech in Cotton Bowl" by Victor Davis, copyright © 1943. Reprinted with permission of the *Dallas Morning News*; "Longhorns Explode Navy Myth, 28–6" by Walter Robertson, copyright © 1964. Reprinted with permission of the *Dallas Morning News*; "Comeback Longhorns Do It Again" by Walter Robertson, copyright © 1970. Reprinted with permission of the *Dallas Morning News*; "Texas Wins Cotton Bowl, 14–12" by Barry Horn, copyright © 1982. Reprinted with permission of the *Dallas Morning News*; "Requiem for an All-American" by Blackie Sherrod, copyright © 2003. Reprinted with permission of the *Dallas Morning News.*